THE COMPLETE SANTA FE

B CKET

LIST

100 Things to Do in Santa Fe Before You Die

by Patricia C. Hodapp

Río Grande Books
Los Ranchos, NM

The Bucket List Book Series

The Basic New Mexico Bucket List by Barbe Awalt (2015)
The Ultimate Hot Air Balloon Bucket List by Barbe Awalt (2015)
The Complete Cowboy Bucket List by Slim Randles (2015)
The Complete Space Buff's Bucket List by Loretta Hall (2016)
The Complete Santa Fe Bucket List by Pat Hodapp (2016)
Kicking the Bucket List by Gail Rubin (2016)
The Complete Green Chile Cheesburger Lovers' Bucket List by Barbe Awalt (2016)
The Complete Crab Lovers' Bucket List by Barbe Awalt (2016)
The Ultimate Christmas Bucket List by Barbe Awalt (2016)

Copyright © 2016 Patricia C. Hodapp
Published by Rio Grande Books
925 Salamanca NW, Los Ranchos, NM 87107 – 5647
(505) 344–9382   www.RioGrandeBooks.com
Printed in the United States of America
Book Design: Paul Rhetts

Library of Congress Cataloging–in–Publication Data

Names: Hodapp, Patricia C.
Title: The complete Santa Fe bucket list : 100 things to do in Santa Fe
before you die / by Patricia C. Hodapp.
Description: Los Ranchos, NM : Rio Grande Books, 2016.
| Series: The bucket list book series
Identifiers: LCCN 2016009902
| ISBN 9781943681099 (pbk. : alk. paper)
Subjects: LCSH: Santa Fe (N.M.)--Guidebooks.
| Santa Fe (N.M.)--Description and travel.
Classification: LCC F804.S23 H67 2016
| DDC 978.9/56--dc23
LC record available at http://lccn.loc.gov/2016009902

Front cover: Adobe wall. Courtesy Paul Rhetts.
Back cover: Inn of Loretto, Santa Fe. Courtesy Creative Commons.

CONTENTS

Acknowledgements

My special thanks to Barbe Awalt and Paul Rhetts for appreciating my love and knowledge of Santa Fe and giving me the opportunity to write the Santa Fe Bucket List. Your encouragement kept me writing and on track.

The friendship, advice, and support of Anne Hillerman and Jamie McGrath Morris have been invaluable.

To Paul and Jonathan whose favorite things and suggestions helped me shape the *100 Things to Do* list.

Many have provided photographs and information to make this book special. My thanks to Maria Clokey, City of Santa Fe Communications/Multi-Media Office, Chelsey Evans, Fred Friedman, Barbe Awalt, Ricardo Cate, Gareth Freeland/Santa Fe Concorso, Kate Nelson, New Mexico History Museum, New Mexico Tourism Department, Dia Winograd, Dave Goldberg, Maria Finley, Sarah Spearman/ Santa Fe Botanical Garden, Roberto E. Rosales, Buffalo Thunder Resort and Casino, Robert Foley, Santa Fe Concert Band, Lolly Martin/Pachamamas, Steve Hansen, Pam Smith, Douglas Wink, Anna Chavez, Michael Benanav, Santa Fe Wine & Chile Fiesta, Folk Art Alliance, Bob Smith, Ski Santa Fe, Morgan Smith, and Luis Sánchez Saturno.

As you read the list of "Near Misses" you will see the depth of wonderful things to enjoy and treasure in Santa Fe. I appreciate all who took the time to share their favorite parts of Santa Fe for this list.

And special thanks to all who shared their top 100 things to do in Santa Fe with me. I hope you agree with my final list.

Pat Hodapp

Patricia C. Hodapp
Director of Libraries

Introduction

The hardest part about creating this *Bucket List* book for Santa Fe was narrowing it down to only 100 things to do. The list could easily be 300 things! As the City Librarian for over a dozen years, I answer questions daily about how to find things in Santa Fe—from chocolate to ice cream, historic sites to shops. When I visited Santa Fe over 40 years ago, I created my own guide to Santa Fe, partly for friends and partly to remember what I loved best about this magical city. Santa Fe is more than just a city, it represents the unique and special part of Northern New Mexico culture, art and people. This list encompasses the greater Santa Fe area, as many "Santa Fe" experiences are within a short drive of Santa Fe, but they exhibit the best of Santa Fe culturally and historically. This list includes what I believe are the best—but I have left a place in the back of the book for you to list your favorites. I have attached a "near misses" list—not that these things are second rate, far from it. I just had to stop somewhere. I make no bones about it, I have made this a personal, "things I like list." But at the same time, those that made the list have been consistently winners in my book for a long time. I tried to select the things that have lingered in my memory and remind me of Santa Fe's best. Many items have website information.

Much of the joy in Santa Fe is discovering those places that have a special meaning to you. Explore and have fun!

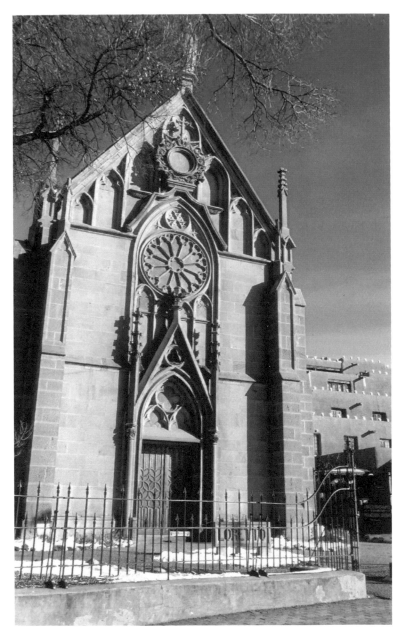

Loretto Chapel. Courtesy Pat Hodapp.

The List:

100. Experience the Plaza

Been to the Plaza? No, not the town square, the Plaza. Since the 1600's there has always been a Plaza at the same site in Santa Fe. Its uses and those who used the Plaza have changed, but it was always a meeting place, a place where one could purchase goods and a place of government. Santa Feans love their Plaza. It is the heart of the city, *el Corazón*. This is the place families go to meet friends and past neighbors, where brides and grooms proudly walk after their wedding in the Basilica. Although many events take place on the Plaza—Indian Market, Pancake Breakfast, Spanish Market, La Fiestas—the real Plaza is just for strolling and meeting up. Santa Feans say you can meet anyone on the Plaza—celebrity, politician, neighbor and even the devil himself. Find a bench, listen to the bandstand music or just sit and read. For New Mexicans you are home, for everyone else this is your new home. *Bienvenidos*!

Center of Santa Fe Plaza. Courtesy Pat Hodapp.

1

99. Look up!

The amazing blue of New Mexico skies with little puffy clouds and skyscraper tall whipped cream clouds rising up over the mountains is a sight you want to share with friends and loved ones. Clouds. Clouds. Clouds. All shapes and sizes. A friend was proposed to in this way. Her sweetheart was in New Mexico on business and he called her as he stood outside the Georgia O'Keeffe Museum and said, " I am looking for a Georgia O'Keeffe, someone who can understand and love the blue and white of New Mexico skies like I do." They got married the next year and they visit Santa Fe often. Recently, Supreme Court Judge Ruth Bader Ginsberg was asked about why she comes to Santa Fe so often—she loves it all but said it is the clouds. They are like nowhere else.

Clouds over the Sangre de Cristo mountains. Courtesy Pat Hodapp.

98. Walk Canyon Road

This one-mile road has hundreds of art galleries and individual artist studios to tour. Canyon Road originally was an Indian foot path, and those who walk it today would say that the road has changed little from that time. Part pavement with narrow 18-inch sidewalks, the Road keeps its old-time appeal. When walking Canyon Road, make sure to check out the gardens behind the galleries; many feature sculptures that cannot be seen from the sidewalk. Check out the Canyon Road Paint Out when dozens of artists take to the Road to paint in plein air. Watch for the Annual Art Feast which pairs restaurants with galleries for special openings—buy your ArtFeast button and ride the free shuttles to Canyon Road and most downtown galleries. Many galleries provide music on Friday nights during the summer and there are restaurants, coffee shops and cafes open into the evenings. No favorites, but if I had my druthers I would end my walk by having tapas and margaritas at El Farol, which claims to be the oldest bar in Santa Fe, and sit where I could look for the many celebrities who come to be a "local" for a night. No asking for a selfie or autograph; Santa Fe prides itself on allowing celebrities to enjoy anonymity.

Canyon Road at Paseo de Peralta. Courtesy Pat Hodapp.

97. Paint!

It is hard to paint in Santa Fe because you want to paint everything! Visit Artisan's art store (2601 Cerrillos Rd.; www.artisan-santafe.com) that has been serving artists for 40 years and pick up art supplies—they have everything from watercolors to pastels to acrylics and more. Take a workshop at the Georgia O'Keeffe Museum (www.okeeffemuseum.org) or just stop and paint what is before you. What a perfect, personalized memento of Santa Fe. Even Georgia O'Keeffe bought some art supplies there—they have her uncashed check to prove it. Artisan's still has a python you can see in its cage—despite hearing that it roams the store at night to keep burglars out — that is an urban legend.

My palette. Courtesy Pat Hodapp.

96. Meet our Farmers

To market, to market! The Farmer's Market (1607 Paseo de Peralta) has a permanent home at the Railyard. The Market features vegetables, fruits, cheeses, jams, baked goods, flowers, honey, eggs and meat. Stroll and select from the fresh organic produce. Inside the building, join the line for coffee and sweet rolls. Stop and enjoy the buskers who sing or play their instruments for your change. Farmers come from all around the state. Peak season for produce is June–October. Also open on Tuesday mornings for a mini-market with the same hours. Come early; you will be competing with restaurants and locals for the freshest products. Seeking local honey, I found Santa Barbara Honey prominently featured. I pointed out to the beekeeper this was a LOCAL farmer's market! He patiently explained to me his bees were on Santa Barbara Drive off Old Pecos Trail, in town. It turns out I could see his hives from our house. Our flowers were feeding his bees! Market hours are 8:00am through 1:00pm. Also check out the Santa Fe Artists Market across the street for great art from local artists. Meet the artists up close and personal.

Farmers Market Honey booth. Courtesy Pat Hodapp.

95. Meet Georgia

This is O'Keeffe Country. Although her homes were in Abiquiu and Ghost Ranch, about an hour north of Santa Fe, the O'Keeffe Museum (214 Johnson St.; www.okeeffemuseum.org) has on display her iconic art. Check the Museum schedule for the exhibits and events; often O'Keeffe's art is paired with other contemporary artists and photographers, such as Ansel Adams. The O'Keeffe Museum events feature artist classes, even for the beginner; children's hands-on art projects, and lectures. I have had the privilege to take workshops with internationally renowned artists such as fiber artist Ted Hallman and Jaune Quick-to-See Smith, a Native American printmaker. On the first Monday of the month is Breakfast with O'Keeffe. The breakfast features many aspects of O'Keeffe's art and the New Mexico country she painted, with knowledgeable speakers, and serves a continental breakfast. Reservations are a must, particularly in the summer months. Stop by Georgia's restaurant (225 Johnson St.; www.georgiassantafe.com) next door for great dining after 4:00 pm. Make it a true Georgia experience: book a tour (www.connect.okeeffemuseum.org/abiquiu-tours) and drive to Abiquiu to tour her home or visit Ghost Ranch to see the landscapes she painted—particularly the Pedernal (flat topped mountain). She stated more than once that God told her if she painted it well enough, it would be hers. Her ashes are scattered on the Pedernal. If planning to take a tour, make sure to book months out. You will be right at the center of O'Keeffe country.

Georgia O'Keeffe Museum. Courtesy Pat Hodapp.

94. Eat a Frito Pie

Love them or hate them, Frito pies are a part of Santa Fe's cuisine. The original recipe says to take an individual–sized bag of Fritos, opening it carefully. Then put in a scoop of red chile, leaving room for chopped onions, jalapenos and shredded cheese on top of the fritos. Often sold for fund raisers, most locals prefer the ones at the Five and Dime on the Plaza (58 East San Francisco St.). Not a favorite of visiting national food critic Anthony Bourdain, who said it feels like "warm crap in a bag." Locals live on them. Even though Bourdain backed down from that comment, locals are unforgiving on the subject. While at the Five and Dime, buy those special gifts for friends. How about a cowboy ashtray or New Mexico salt and pepper shakers or a bandana or just about anything with Santa Fe printed on it. A true Five & Dime store.

Frito pie. Courtesy Pat Hodapp.

93. Honor Our Veterans

The Baatan Museum and Library (1050 Old Pecos Trail; www.baatanmuseum.com) honors the 1,800 men from New Mexico who were taken captive by the Japanese in 1942 on the island of Bataan in World War II. After the brutal death march and three years of captivity, less than half of these soldiers would return home. The Bataan Memorial Military Museum and Library is dedicated to the memory of these New Mexico soldiers and their families. You will find military manuscripts in the library and over 30,000 military artifacts in the museum. It is a moving experience to meet a veteran of WWII, and particularly a survivor of the death march, in Santa Fe at the Museum or at the Veteran's Day Parade and ceremony. Few veterans are left, but those who are still with us appreciate our recognition of their sacrifice for us.

The Baatan Museum. Courtesy Pat Hodapp.

92. Do the Santa Fe Indian Market

This is the big one. People come from across the United States and Europe to visit and enjoy the art at this gathering of artists. Over 1,000 Native American artists show on the Plaza and surrounding streets (www.swaia.org). Aficionados of a particular artist's work line up in front of the artist's tent before dawn to be the first in line to purchase the art. Even special youth tents draw collectors early. Parking is expensive and hard to come by. Galleries hold openings for their artists the week before and during Indian Market weekend. Most are free and they welcome visitors. In late August, come and enjoy the crowds, art, entertainment, Navajo tacos, and do serious crowd watching. Oh, did I mention the word *expensive*? No bartering, no haggling. This art is world class.

Indigenous Fine Art Market (www.ifam.org), a recent spin-off of Native American artists, holds a market in the Railyard just before Indian Market, on Thursday through Saturday. Winter Indian Market is held over Thanksgiving weekend in Santa Fe at the Community Convention Center.

Santo Domingo/Kewa artist jewelry booth. Courtesy Pat Hodapp.

91. Walk Art Fridays

The first Friday of the month year-round, galleries on Palace Street, just off the Plaza, hold receptions for their new artists. The museums, Georgia O'Keeffe (www.okeeffemuseum.org), the New Mexico Museum of Art (www.nmartmuseum.org) and the New Mexico History Museum (nmhistorymuseum.org), are free from 5:00 pm to closing. The NM Museum of Art offers music, from jazz to country, on first Fridays in their courtyard in warm months. Most of the galleries are located on Palace and Lincoln, just off the Plaza. Listen for the mariachis playing on the balcony of the Manitou Galleries on the corner of Palace and Sheridan. Enjoy wine, sparkling water and snacks. Sorry, no strolling on the street with wine.

Also stroll the fourth Friday in the Railyard, at Guadalupe and Paseo de Peralta, for top modern gallery openings.

First Friday Gallery walk. Courtesy Pat Hodapp.

90. Cook up a New Mexican Recipe

The Santa Fe School of Cooking (125 North Guadalupe; www.santafeschoolofcooking.com) offers culinary classes featuring foods of the Southwest. You will make such favorites as fried squash blossoms, enchiladas, and flan—then eat what you made! Keep the recipes to master at home and wow your friends. Also has a restaurant and gift shop.

Santa Fe School of Cooking. Courtesy Pat Hodapp.

89. Shop for Christmas Early

The Christmas Shop (116 E. Palace St.; www.susanschrist-masshop.com) is a Christmas store that prides itself on its special ornaments and decorations. Hand-blown glass ornaments of the many churches in New Mexico are a favorite collectible, as well as pottery, Nativity sets and straw ornaments. My favorite Jemez pottery Nativity set has Joseph and Mary with the baby Jesus wrapped in a cornhusk in the manger. Very New Mexican.

Nativities of the Southwest by Susan Topp Weber. Courtesy Pat Hodapp.

88. Enjoy music – TGIF

Every Friday at 5:30 pm, the First Presbyterian Church, at the corner of Grant and Marcy Streets, holds a half-hour concert. A perfect way to end your week or start your Friday night gallery walks and dinner out. Concerts feature local and national artists, from organists to violinists to ensembles who present the best in classical music. The programs are free but donations are always welcome. The church is a restored John Gaw Meem design. When the power went off one Friday night in a rain storm, the pianist and soloist performed by candle light. Only in Santa Fe.

First Presbyterian Church. Courtesy Pat Hodapp.

87. Get Your Chocolate Fix

Visitors always ask about chocolate. A traditional chocolate featuring Aztec–style chocolate drinks can be found at Kakawa chocolate shop (1050 Paseo de Peralta; www.Kakawachocolates.com). Small cups of all shapes and decoration hold such delectable chocolate drinks as rose petal chocolate and of course, chile chocolate. Truly this is the drink of the (Aztec) gods. Don't miss Señor Murphy's on Old Santa Fe Trail next to La Fonda (www.Senormurphys.com; and 177 Paseo de Peralta in the De Vargas Mall). Señor Murphy's features pinon nuts in chocolate candy and pinon caramel logs. Great for a treat for a hostess, or to take to the office back home or just keep a sack for yourself in case your hotel does not put a chocolate on your pillow.

Chocolate treats at Kakawa's. Courtesy Pat Hodapp.

86. Bike or Hike Santa Fe

The Santa Fe Century (www.SantafeCentury.com)every May brings over 2,600 bicyclists to Santa Fe to ride 100 miles around Santa Fe County on a street course. Check their website for various rides. Bicycling is popular, but riding on the city streets is still challenging. It is always wise to check out your planned ride ahead of time – some bike lanes end suddenly or are so narrow you might feel uncomfortable to bike them. Mountain biking attracts bicyclists to trails around Santa Fe. Mellow Velo (132 E. Marcy St.; www.Mellowvelo. com) rents bicycles of all sizes. Need bike repairs? Check out Rob and Charlie's (1632 St. Michael's Dr.; www.robandcharlie's.com). Bicycle paths go through most of Santa Fe. Feel like hiking? Trails abound around Santa Fe, from gentle walks to strenuous hikes. Be prepared as Santa Fe weather can change in a minute. Remember you are at high altitude, drink lots of water, dress in layers and bring food. Snow has been spotted as late as July at the highest elevations. The city's Dale Ball Trail, which heads along Hyde Park Road on the way to the ski basin, has great spots to watch the golden aspen in the fall. Look for Aspen Vista, picnic areas for parking and a trailhead. The city maintains over 30 miles of trails in the city and the foothills of the Sangre de Cristo mountains. Two parking lots were built to serve Dale Ball Trail hikers: one off of Hyde Park Road where it intersects Sierra del Norte, and another at the intersection of Upper Canyon Road and Cerro Gordo. Additionally, parking can be found at St. John's College and along Camino Cruz Blanca, which is the closest parking to access Atalaya Trail. Many guided tours are also offered. — Tourism Santa Fe, www.santafe.org; www. Santafewalkabouts.com

Avid city bicyclist. Courtesy Pat Hodapp.

Santa Fe hiking trail. Courtesy City of Santa Fe Communications/Multi-Media Office.

85. Read

The city used to have more bookstores per capita than any other city in the US. There are still many independent book stores, each with its own special stock of books. The Friends of the Santa Fe Public Library has two used book shops, one in the Main Library (145 Washington Ave.) and one at the Southside Branch (6599 Jaguar Dr.). Books, vinyl records, CDs and DVDs sell at rock-bottom prices. About a dozen times a year, the public library branches host book sales – thousands of donated books are sold to benefit the library's purchasing of new books and other projects. It's a great time to stock up on paperbacks for travel or by the pool. — www. santafelibrary.org

Santa Fe Public Library book sale. Courtesy Pat Hodapp.

84. Walk the Walk of Fame

Santa Fe's own Walk of Fame honors artists with brass plaques set in the sidewalk along Palace Avenue, between Lincoln and Sheridan Avenues, in front of the NM Museum of Art. Eighteen names are memorialized including Oliver La Farge, Willa Cather, Lew Wallace, Maria Martinez and Georgia O'Keeffe. Because it was created and installed in 1990, many more recent New Mexican authors and artists are not included in the walk, such as Tony Hillerman, Hampton Sides, Rudolfo Anaya, Michael McGarrity, Cormac McCarthy and George R.R. Martin. As much as I am thrilled to write this Santa Fe Bucket list book, I don't think I qualify for my own name plaque.

Plaque honoring Oliver LaFarge. Courtesy Pat Hodapp.

83. Meet the Local Artists

In late June, close to 75 artists and over 40 studios open their studios to the public in a two-weekend event, the Santa Fe Studio Tour (www.santafestudiotour.com). The artists' work includes molded and blown glass, wood carving, weavings, and all types of paintings. It's an opportunity to meet the artists and discuss their work. Most studios offer refreshments. Other art shows are open weekends during warm weather. Check out the Santa Fe Artists Market (www.santafesocietyofartists.com) at the Railyard at Guadalupe and Paseo de Peralta, which is usually open the same hours as the Farmers' Market on Saturdays, 8:00 am–1:00 pm. And the Cathedral Park has juried shows. The Santa Fe Society Artists are under tents right downtown on San Francisco Street, one block west of the Plaza. Great art at reasonable prices from local artists.

Street Art Show. Courtesy Pat Hodapp.

82. Visit 109 E. Palace

109 E. Palace was the face to the world for incoming scientists and other workers for the Manhattan Project in Los Alamos, "up the hill" as locals describe it. From 1943 through the dropping the bombs on Japan in 1945 and the end of the war, secrecy was the byword throughout the WWII project. Project director Robert Oppenheimer developed and designed the first nuclear bomb in Los Alamos. Workers at Los Alamos were greeted and checked in at 109 E. Palace and that was the only address they had until they left the project. Visitors come to see the office in the back of a pottery and gift shop. Nearby was the Castillo Bridge that was over the Santa Fe River, where Soviet spy Klaus Fuchs met to hand off secret data on the nuclear bomb to agent Harry Gold in 1945. This allowed the Soviets to speed up their work, being able to create their bomb two years sooner. Documents revealed a key signal between Gold and his Soviet agent was a Jello™ box.

109 E. Palace Ave. Courtesy Pat Hodapp.

81. Boo the Villains!

The annual Santa Fe melodrama, performed at the Santa Fe Playhouse (www.santafeplayhouse.org) at 142 De Vargas Street, is a Santa Fe tradition. Held in September leading up to Fiestas, the playwrights and local wags concoct a melodrama to skewer most of Santa Fe's politicos and any and all events from the past year. The humor is sometimes juvenile, but then the topics they are skewering are juvenile and truly show why Santa Fe is called the City Different. The playhouse offers year-round classic plays and plays from new playwrights.

Theatre goers at the Santa Fe Playhouse. Courtesy Pat Hodapp.

80. Flap those Jacks

The annual 4th of July Pancake Breakfast on the Plaza (www.pancakesontheplaza.com) begins at 7:00am and goes until noon. Join your friends and make new ones while enjoying the famous pancakes, ham, strawberries, orange juice and coffee. Get there early, as lines will form all the way across the Plaza—over 7,000 people have attended. Music is played from the bandstand and local sponsors have booths and giveaways. Everyone needs another reusable shopping bag or water bottle! A silent auction is also held. A vintage car show and arts and crafts booths add to the festivities. The Pancake Breakfast benefits the Santa Fe Rotary's public service projects. Sorry, usually no dogs are allowed on the Plaza for this event.

Pancake Breakfast mascot. Courtesy City of Santa Fe Communications/ Multi-Media Office.

79. Enjoy Sunrise, Sunset

Walk to the Cross of the Martyrs to see the sun rise. This spot draws locals and tourists to the cross that honors the martyred Franciscan priests and settlers killed in the Pueblo Indian uprising in 1680. Walk up to it off Paseo de Peralta, a strenuous stairway, or enter off Artist Road and Fort Marcy Park. Your view of Santa Fe is a 360 degree one. About a mile away, on Paseo de la Loma, is an earlier cross off a cul de sac. Known to few, this cross is rarely visited. Sunsets in New Mexico are such an amazing mix of colors and cloud shapes, truly artists cannot capture them as they really look.

The best thing to do is to find a beautiful spot and watch the sunset in front of you. The Sangre de Cristo mountains on the east side of Santa Fe got their name, which means blood of Christ, from the pink afterglow at sunset. Most evenings, you can soak up the glow as the sun sets. One favorite place of locals is the La Fonda Hotel Bell Tower (100 E. San Francisco St.; www.LaFondahotel.com). Make sure to get to the fifth floor Bell Tower long before sunset, just to see the view of Santa Fe. Then settle into the chairs, and order your favorite beverage and snacks, and wait for the sunset. Only open in the summer, call (505) 982-5511 to see when it is open.

Santa Fe sunset. Courtesy Pat Hodapp.

Cross of the Martyrs. Courtesy Pat Hodapp.

78. Walk the Arroyos With Care

Meandering through the hills and fields are arroyos, known elsewhere as gullies. They are the perfect place to walk your dog on the sandy soil or sit on the banks and think of the many who have travelled in New Mexico. Look for deer tracks and also mountain lion tracks! A friend found a pottery shard, evidence of Indians having camped nearby. But the clear paths are brushed clean by raging water pouring down out of the foothills and mountains after rains. It may be clear where you are, but afternoon rains may be blasting the mountains above you, with all the rain being funneled into seemingly innocent, peaceful arroyos. Arroyos in Santa Fe have been known to rise to 6–8 feet in a flood in minutes. Take care, choose your arroyo carefully. Monsoons come in early July; no we are not kidding, rain and often hail can dump up to 2 inches of rain and several inches of hail in minutes and also flood streets and trails. Just be prepared.

Water scrubbed arroyo. Courtesy Pat Hodapp.

77. Are you Ready for Spanish Market?

Over 200 adult and youth artists show traditional Spanish art at this market that is held on the Plaza and surrounding streets. The festival takes part over the weekend, usually the last weekend in July. Learn the difference between *santos* and *bultos*. Be amazed by the fine straw art. Check out the winners of the Best in Show. Entertainment and food booths are available in the Plaza area. Then explore Hispanic contemporary art. Contemporary Hispanic Market (www.contemporaryhispanicmarketinc.com) brings over 130 artists who work in a contemporary Hispanic style. Held in late July coinciding with the Traditional Spanish Market (www.spanishcolonial.org), it kicks off with a reception at the Santa Fe Community Convention Center (Marcy at Grant St.) on Friday night before the weekend market.

Spanish Market artists under the portal. Courtesy City of Santa Fe Communications/Multi-Media Office.

76. Visit the Loretto Chapel and the Miraculous Staircase

When the Loretto Chapel (207 Old Santa Fe Trail; www.lorettochapel.com/staircase.html) was built by the Sisters of Loretto in the late 1800s, they had no way to get to the choir loft and a regular stairway would take too much room. As an answer to their prayers, a carpenter appeared and created the staircase in corkscrew manner using no nails or support. This miraculous staircase's carpenter then disappeared. Legend is that the carpenter was St. Joseph; however, two families in Santa Fe claim that the mysterious carpenter was a relative of theirs. The mystery continues. The chapel is a wonderful venue for many musical groups in Santa Fe as well as weddings.

The Loretto Chapel's Miraculous Staircase. Courtesy of New Mexico Tourism Department.

75. Indulge with Ice Cream or Gelato

Taos Cow: what a great name for ice cream. This ice cream is almost local – the cows live in Taos. It is considered one of the top ice creams by aficionados. Taos Cow ice cream is worth searching for. It is served at Shake Foundation, and limited flavors can be found at C.G. Higgins Chocolate Shop (www.cghiggins.com) at 130 Lincoln Street. It is worth every penny. When the new Archbishop of Santa Fe was installed, his first question was "Where can I get great ice cream?" Taos Cow, of course. Also sample the gelato, the specialty at ECCO (128 E. Marcy St.; www.eccogelato.com), a friendly coffee and gelato shop. The treats are made fresh daily and Matt and his crew give samples of all their many flavors. Try the coffee and chocolate hazelnut, and the pistachio and, and... For the more daring, try the habanero–strawberry, cool and refreshing with just a hint of heat. One hot summer day when the power went out on the street, ECCO tried to close but some of us convinced the staff to let us get our gelato fix first.

ECCO Gelato Shop. Courtesy Pat Hodapp.

74. Hail the Santa Fe Pick-Up or a Pedicab

Shop until you drop, then take the free Santa Fe Pick–Up
— (505) 231–2573; www.takethetrails.com. These vans circle
the city from the train station to Canyon Road to downtown
and back, every thirty minutes, Monday through Sunday
from 10:00am to 5:30pm. Check out the Historic District
shuttle. Look for the "Pick–It Up Here" sign. Or hail a pedi-
cab! — (505) 577–5056; www.santafepedicabs.com. This
rickshaw–like ride is a godsend when going from art gallery
to lunch to Canyon Road to your hotel. The pedal masters
are friendly and knowledgeable about Santa Fe. They are
available for historic tours or weddings. The price of a ride
will not break the bank–most trips are very reasonable. Note
they do not go outside of the downtown area, so no rides to
Ten Thousand Waves. Relax and leave the pedaling (or driving) to them!

Santa Fe Pick-Up van. Courtesy Pat Hodapp.

73. Visit the Museum of Contemporary Native Art

The mission of the Institute of American Indian Arts (IAIA) Musem of Contemporary Native Arts (108 Cathedral Pl.; www.iaia.edu/museum) advances Native art through exhibits, collections and public programs. It presents the best in today's contemporary Native American arts. Check their website for special shows and guest speakers. The museum is staffed by young Native Americans who also often are artists. A great opportunity to discuss their art and experience their enthusiastic commitment to their art and their culture. The changing painting of the log poles along the façade on Cathedral Place seems to represent the changing modern Indian art and point of view. I love going by the painted poles on my daily commute. The art is both playful and serious at the same time. It is a popular place for a selfie.

Museum of Contemporary Native Art. Courtesy Pat Hodapp.

72. Defend Your Green Chile Cheeseburger

Competition is tough in the New Mexico favorite green chile cheeseburger arena; there is even a Santa Fe Green Chile Cheeseburger Smackdown (www.santafe.org/Fun_Food_Event/). Everyone has their favorite bar or restaurant's green chile cheeseburger on their list. It is not just a good burger with green chile piled on top, oh no. The proportions need to be just right, from hand-selected meat (beef or buffalo?), the right kind of green chile grilled to perfection, and don't even start to argue about the kind of cheese! Try the Cowgirl's buffalo, bacon, cheese or beef, bacon, cheese with green chile (www.cowgirlssantafe.com). My hands-down favorite is Santa Fe Bite (www.sfbite.com), making hand-shaped burgers from fresh ground beef since 1952. Yum. To the aficionado, it is science and love. Throughout New Mexico there are hundreds of recipes – there is even a Green Chile Cheeseburger Trail (www.newmexico.org/trails/green-chile-cheeseburger-trail/) where you can traverse the state only eating the best of GCCs! Try them all!

Santa Fe Bite's Delux Green Chile Cheeseburger. Courtesy Pat Hodapp.

71. See a Flick

Alternative, small eclectic theatres provide the best in films, and Santa Fe boasts many venues. As a bonus, you might see George R. R. Martin of *Game of Thrones* fame at his Jean Cocteau Cinema (jeancocteaucinema.com) or directors and filmmakers at these theatres. Martin made a splash when he brought a real, live wolf to promote *Game of Thrones* at his theatre. The wolf came from the Wild Spirit Wolf Sanctuary in Ramah, NM, where you can camp and see wolves saved from many kinds of challenges, humans and nature. These are not wolf–dogs, they are the real thing. One of the wolves was brought to the Santa Fe Public Library for a children's program. There was not a sound when the wolf and his handler entered the room. The wolf took in the room, with its Paul Newman blue eyes, and lay down to keep an eye on us. Trust me, we did not move. The usually rowdy children's crowd was verrrry respectful. Other venues are The Screen at 1600 St. Michael's Dr. (www.thescreensf.com) and The CCA at 1050 Old Pecos Trail (www.ccasantafe.org).

Jean Cocteau Cinema. Courtesy Pat Hodapp.

70. Strike up the Music

The Santa Fe Concert Band (www.facebook.com/San-taFeConcertBand) is a mainstay for presenting concerts for holidays and special occasions on the lawn of the Federal Park next to the Federal Courthouse. Get pumped with Sousa and show tunes! Bring chairs or blankets and pack a lunch. Their Christmas carol sing–a–long draws families to the Lensic Theatre (www.lensic.com) for a warm, sharing, homey event. Everyone dresses in holiday attire – little girls in velvet and bows and boys in button-down shirts and vests. But come as you are – you will find yourself singing and getting the holiday spirit.

The Santa Fe Symphony Orchestra and Chorus (www.santafesymphony.org), formerly a volunteer group, has become a full–fledged classical orchestra and chorale ensemble presenting a full schedule of programs. Do not miss their performance of the Messiah, scheduled the Sunday of Thanksgiving weekend at the Lensic. Under the spell of the music you will bond with the people next to you.

Santa Fe Concert Band, Federal Park. Courtesy Robert Foley.

69. Dish it Up

Nambe® ware was developed by Los Alamos scientists. The iconic serving bowls, plates, vases and tableware have a contemporary design, yet are so durable and useful, they can go from freezer to oven. The silvery metal is unique, like silver, but sturdier. When a friend was dating, she talked so much about how she loved her Nambe®, the boyfriend thought she was talking about her dog! When they got married, Nambe® was where she registered for presents. Locals know the secret of Nambe®'s annual discontinued and seconds sale. Join the crowds who flock to the sale for their fix of Nambe® ware (Paseo de Peralta at Canyon Rd. and 10 W. San Francisco St.; www.nambe.com).

Nambe® ware bowl. Courtesy Pat Hodapp.

68. Enjoy 7 Days of Breakfast in Santa Fe

New Mexicans love their breakfast – any time of day. Politicos, businessmen and all who know about the restaurant meet at Tia Sofia's for great northern New Mexican food. We're talking everything smothered in red or green — enchiladas, huevos rancheros and of course, the New Mexican staple, the breakfast burrito. Or try Angel's Bakery & Café for fresh baked pastries – fruit filled empanadas, croissants, cinnamon rolls plus a full menu of breakfast burritos and red and green on everything, except the pastries! Café Pasquale has veggie, vegan, organic, and it is all delicious. The favorite of many native New Mexicans is The Plaza Café. That is where they meet their friends from their neighborhood and the past. Many a Santa Fean gathered with family after a birth in the family, special birthdays and of course the Prom. Many in a hurry just grab a hand–held burrito, the original quick breakfast. Tortilla Flats sounds like a chain restaurant, but this restaurant is New Mexican right down to staff who have been there for years. You will dream about their breakfast plates like their breakfast burrito. As our friend Fred says, it would feed an army and still have leftovers to take home! La Fonda Hotel's restaurant La Plazuela looks formal, but is informal. Reba McIntire recently ate there TWICE in one day. Santa Feans waited patiently for Tecolote Café to find a new home in 2015—it's open, hurrah! I have to confess once when living in Denver, a friend and I drove to Santa Fe for breakfast, walked the Plaza and drove back. There is something about Santa Fe breakfasts. Here is my list of seven days of heavenly breakfasts.

Day 1: Tia Sophia's, 210 W. San Francisco St.

Day 2: Café Pasqual, 121 Don Gaspar (www.pasquals.com) (I'd make reservations for any meal…)

Day 3: Angel's Bakery & Café, 125 E. Water St.

Day 4: The Plaza Café, 54 Lincoln Ave. (www. thefamousplazacafe.com)

Day 5: Tortilla Flats, 3139 Cerrillos Rd. (www.tortillaflats. com)

Day 6: La Plazuela at La Fonda (www.lafondasantafe.com/ la-plazuela)

Day 7: Tecolote Café, 1616 St. Michael's Dr. (www. tecolotecafe.com)

Tia Sophia's breakfast enchiladas. Courtesy Pat Hodapp.

67. Visit the Roundhouse

Not your typical gold–domed capitol building, the Roundhouse is a round, Pueblo kiva-style design. One political wag claims it was built in the round so politicians could not be cornered. Explore the Governor's Art Gallery and the sculptures placed around the building on the Capitol Grounds (Paseo de Peralta at Old Santa Fe Trail). The art in the gallery features all aspects of NM art – from oils to acrylics to sculpture. The mission of the Capitol Art Foundation is to collect, preserve, exhibit and interpret works of art by New Mexico artists and other relevant works of art that reflect the rich and varied history, cultures and art forms of the state. The Capitol Art Foundation is committed to public education programs that address the needs of a diverse audience and seeks to promote goodwill and understanding through its programs. My favorite show was Carlotta Boettcher's car hoods painted with scenes of New Mexico. Beautifully executed and an homage to Northern New Mexico car culture.

The Capitol building is open Monday through Friday 8:00am–5:30pm, and Saturdays after Memorial Day and before Labor Day. Tours of the building are given regularly throughout the year and can be arranged by calling (505) 986–4589. For more information about visiting the Capitol building, go to www.nmlegis.gov/lcs/.

The Roundhouse, New Mexico's State Capitol. Courtesy Pat Hodapp.

66. Is it Art or a Car?

The Southwest's premier automotive gathering is the Santa Fe Concorso (www.Santafeconcorso.com) held in late September at the Club at Las Campanas, off Route 599 just 15 minutes north of Santa Fe. Showcasing over 100 rare and exotic cars and motorcycles,the Concorso's main event is at the Las Campanas Sunrise Golf Club on the 9th Fairway on Sunday. Saturday of the weekend, the vehicles drive to the Santa Fe Plaza. It is a grand parade of sporty, luxury, and elegant vehicles. Enjoy the show on the Plaza, and talk to owners and drivers about what it takes to own show cars. Look at such rare cars as a 1936 Delahaze, 1964 Ferrari 250 LM, 1959 Alfa Romeo Spider Volce, 1925 Bugatti, plus American cars and motorcycles. I can relate to the beautiful show cars. I had a 1969 rebuilt and restored Alfa Romeo Beretta that was not a glamorous show car, but could beat any car off the line. Since it is past the statute of limitations, I can share that I took it to 120 mph when I owned it. I can only imagine what it is like to drive a Bugatti or Ferrari. Tickets range from $50 to $150 for the event or enjoy the free parade show of cars on the Plaza.

Concorso festivities. Courtesy Garret Vreeland.

65. Say Boo!

The original ghost tour of Santa Fe (www.theoriginalsantafeghosttour.weebly.com) has been led by Peter Sinclaire for over forty years. He loves to take you to his favorite haunts. This storyteller will keep you listening to him and for such supernatural sounds as the moans and cries of La Llorona by the river. Want a walking tour of historical Santa Fe? Check at the New Mexico History Museum (www.nmhistorymuseum.org). Museum guides will take you on historical Santa Fe tours weekdays.

New Mexico History Museum blue doors. Courtesy Pat Hodapp.

64. Eat Al Fresco

Enjoy the pleasure of Santa Fe's wonderful weather by eating on a patio. When checking out a restaurant, ask if they have patio seating or an outdoor deck. Not all are visible from the street. Meet friends and share a special meal. My personal favorite is Casa Sena, set in a courtyard off Palace Avenue's portal; it is like eating in Monet's garden. Gardeners tend the wild growth of flowers with love – some have gardened there 20 years. Enter off the East Palace Avenue portal and enjoy the instant shade of old trees. This 1796 hacienda was the home of Mexican Army Major Jose Sena and his family. Today, tables set outside provide a romantic setting any time of day or night. No matter how tempting, don't pick bouquets of flowers like one local did to have a floral extravaganza at her home for her dinner guests. In typical Santa Fe style, the restaurant did not charge her or chastise her and welcomed her back when she dined there again.

Al fresco at Cowgirl's patio. Courtesy Pat Hodapp.

63. Botanical Garden in Santa Fe?

Being in a high desert climate, you will be amazed to see the number of beautiful native plants and flowers that have been grown in the Botanical Garden (715 Camino Lejo; www.santafebotanicalgarden.org). Not just cactus. A recent addition to the many museums in Santa Fe, this is a living museum. Projects are offered for children on gardening, and adults flock to the Botanical Garden for ideas for their dry, desert gardens. A special light show, *Glow*, is displayed over the Christmas holidays. Living in Santa Fe in about year 9 of a 20-year drought, most Santa Feans have learned to love cactus, native grasses, Russian sage and lavender. Those fields and gardens that are all showy with a purple flower in July through September most likely are Russian Sage (and it is neither Russian or sage!) A few foolhardy Santa Feans live in denial and pay thousands of dollars for their water bills to waste our water on their idea of a Midwestern garden where rain and water are plentiful. My mother would have said that they will sure miss that water when they are in hell.

Santa Fe Botanical Garden. Courtesy Santa Fe Botanical Garden.

62. Which Can I Eat?

Vigas, virga, latilla or *natilla*? Easy, have a *natilla* for dessert. This light and creamy dessert is made from whipped egg whites and egg custard. *Virga* is the trailing rain that floats like a veil below a storm, and never touches the ground. *Vigas* are the huge poles that hold up the ceiling or a *ramada* or *pergola*. The *latilla* are smaller logs, often peeled aspen or spruce, that the *vigas* hold up, either for a ceiling or an outside *ramada* or *pergola*. Got that? Now, I'll have a *natilla*, thank you.

Natilla dessert. Courtesy Pat Hodapp.

61. Feel the Drums

There are many Indian Pow Wows, gatherings of tribes, around the state and in Santa Fe, but my favorite is at the Santa Fe Indian School's Fall Festival (1501 Cerrillos Rd.; www.sfis.k12.nm.us).

It's not the largest Pow Wow, but one that makes your heart beat faster when you hear the drums and the Native Americans calling out to the beat. Watch the dancers, many young children, in tribal dress taking part. You can feel the drums in your bones. At most public dances you can take pictures or sketch, but not at the pueblos. Show respect of pueblo culture. Best to ask permission before taking pictures or risk having your camera or cellphone confiscated. One hot summer day, I was tired of the paperwork at work and took a walk. In the distance I could hear drumming, and as it came closer my heart started to beat to the rhythm. The music? The drumming and chanting was coming from a boom box in a low rider car. I returned to work with tapping feet.

Pow Wow dancer. Courtesy New Mexico Tourism Department.

60. Catch a Show

The Lensic Performing Arts Center (211 W. San Francisco St.; www.lensic.com) is Santa Fe's premier theatre and arts center, hosting over 250 events a year. Built in 1931, this grand movie place was a gift from Nathan Salmon, a Syrian merchant who made his fortune in Santa Fe. The theatre built in Spanish style kept Santa Feans entertained throughout the depression. Naming the movie palace was done with a contest—the name had to be made up of a family's first name initials. Lensic was chosen, and by luck, the first part of the name was "lens." Classic films are presented inexpensively; $5 to see the old *King Kong,* or the cult classic *Dirty Dancing?* for free! How can you refuse? On the music side, enjoy such luminaries as Art Garfunkle, kd lang, and the Live Met Opera simulcast. The Lannan Foundation also presents a series of authors and poets. Restored in the 1990s by the Zeckendorf family, the movie palace plays on.

The Lensic Performing Arts Center. Courtesy Pat Hodapp.

59. See the Stars

No, not Hollywood stars, real stars in the sky. Just above Santa Fe, you can see stars and planets that are hidden in most of the country due to light pollution. Drive up Hyde Park Road and stop at any park or camp ground and get out your telescope. Or join Astronomy Adventures (www. AstronomyAdventures.com) any time of year to see the night sky filled with bright stars and planets. Telescopes are provided.

Clear skies. Courtesy Roberto E. Rosales.

58. Stop in the La Fonda Hotel

Histories have shown us that since 1821 a hotel, and most likely some kind of traveller's stop even earlier than that, has been at the corner of Old Santa Fe Trail and San Francisco Street, anchoring the Plaza. Fred Harvey leased the hotel in 1926 and the Harvey Girls of train fame served food at Harvey Hotels along the train route. Everyone has come to see celebrities or been seen. Just settle into one of the leather chairs in the lobby and soak in the ambiance. The guest register at La Fonda on the Plaza (www.lafondasantafe.com) includes the names of Gen. and Mrs. Ulysses S. Grant, Thornton Wilder, Jimmy Stewart, Errol Flynn and Diane Keaton. The restaurant and bar are favorites of locals and tourists alike. Ask to see the bullet holes in one of the *vigas*!

La Fonda Hotel. Courtesy Pat Hodapp.

57. What is With the Blue?

Houses in Northern New Mexico sport many shades of blue paint on window frames and doorways. It is believed to keep the owners safe from witches, known as *brujas*. It is believed this tradition traces back to the Moorish influence on the Spanish who brought the superstition to New Mexico.

Blue doors. Courtesy Pat Hodapp.

56. Visit St. Francis de Assisi Basilica

The St. Francis Cathedral (231 Cathedral Pl.; www.cbsfa. org), now a Basilica, was built starting in 1869, in the Romanesque style popular in Bishop Lamy's home country of France. A side adobe chapel is the home to La Conquistadora, a statue of the Virgin Mary that was carried into Santa Fe in 1693 by Don Diego De Vargas in the reconquest of the city of Santa Fe from the Indians. This statue is clothed daily in special dresses and shoes made by local seamstresses. A procession takes La Conquistadora from the Cathedral to Rosario Chapel. The procession is made up of devout La Fiesta Council members and parishioners. Next door is the Cathedral Park. This shady park is welcoming on Santa Fe's hot days. Many juried art shows are held here in the summer. Choose a bench and people watch or just read. Listen for the bells. The Basilica of St. Francis, just East of the Plaza, rings its bells throughout the day. I had friends who visited London and when I asked them what did they think of Big Ben's ringing bells, they realized they had never stopped to listen. Sorry, no dogs allowed in the park.

Basilica of San Francisco de Assisi. Courtesy Pat Hodapp.

55. See SITE Santa Fe

An innovative, contemporary art gallery, SITE Santa Fe (1606 Paseo de Peralta; www.sitesantafe.org) opened in 1995. Since then the gallery has hosted dozens of exhibits and installations and hosted an art and cultural series of lectures. SITE Santa Fe supports contemporary art and cultural production of the Americas. Artist talks and student nights add to the broad range of exciting projects at the SITE. Don't expect the usual; this cutting edge gallery puts art right in your face for you to figure out.

SITE Santa Fe. Courtesy Barbe Awalt.

54. Admire Turquoise and Heishi

Turquoise is like a piece of New Mexico's sky. It varies in color from palest blue to green and the Cerrillos turquoise was mined south of Santa Fe. The Navajo perfected the styles of turquoise jewelry in belts, rings and necklaces paired with silver. Heishi (hee shee) are beads traditionally of shell, but today turquoise and coral are among the other materials that are hand-ground, shaped flat like a wagon wheel and strung into necklaces. True heishi beads are so smooth the strands will roll in your hand like a smooth snake. Santo Domingo/Kewa Pueblo jewelry makers are known for their fine bead work. Many of the Palace of the Governor Portal Indian artists are from Santa Domingo/Kewa.

Heishi and silver jewelry. Courtesy Pat Hodapp.

53. Ski Santa Fe

At 12,000 feet, Ski Santa Fe (www.skisantafe.com) is one of the highest ski slopes in the US. There are great runs for beginning through expert skiers and snowboarders in its 680 acres. Take the super quad ski lift in late summer through mid–October to see fall foliage and hike. Ski Santa Fe is eighteen miles north of Santa Fe. Don't want to drive? Take the Mountain Trail Ski Shuttle (www.ridethebluebus.com) to Ski Santa Fe. It leaves the South Capitol Railrunner station and other downtown stops as early as 8:00 am. $5.00 per trip, and the ticket cost can be taken off the price of your lift ticket.

Ski Santa Fe chairlift. Courtesy of Ski Santa Fe.

52. Dance!

Santa Fe is home to the internationally acclaimed Maria Benitez Institute for Spanish Arts flamenco school. Benitez's students perform at many venues around the city. Professional performances abound in Santa Fe. One night, just off the Plaza, I could hear rhythmic tapping heels and a guitar being played. A local hotel had an impromptu performance outside on their street side patio. People were crowding the sidewalk and street to watch and listen. Music and dancing at its best. For regular performances, check such venues as El Farol (808 Canyon Rd.; www.elfarolsf.com) and The Lodge at Santa Fe (750 N. St. Francis; www.lodgeatsantafe.com).

Flamenco dancers at El Rancho de las Golondrinas. Courtesy Barbe Awalt.

51. Explore Museum Hill

Situated on a hill just 3 miles southeast of downtown Santa Fe are four museums—the International Folk Art Museum (www.internationalfolkart.org), Spanish Colonial Arts Museum (www.spanishcolonial.org/museum), Museum of Indian Arts and Culture (www.IndianArtsandCulture.org), and the Wheelwright Museum (www.wheelwright.org).

Each gathers together a part of Santa Fe's history and international exhibits, from Native Americans to Spanish history to folk art to Indian jewelry. The new installation at the Wheelwright Museum of an original trading post has added a new exhibit to take in. Visitors take to the International Folk Art Museum's exhibits like a kid in a candy store; the collection is exhaustive.

Enjoy the view from Milner Plaza and leave time to stop in the special shops and the Museum Hill Café (www.museumhillcafe.net). The Café hosts music weekends, check out the website. Each museum hosts a gift shop that has jewelry, weavings and great selections of books on the Southwest.

The Wheelwright hosts free storytelling every Saturday and Sunday evening in August by beloved story teller Joe Hayes. No one can resist stories such as *The Day It Rained Tortillas*. Check out the sculpture garden and native plants. Walk the labyrinth or just enjoy the incredible views.

All are located in the 700 block of Camino Lejo.

Museum Hill Rain Dancer statue. Courtesy Pat Hodapp.

50. Billy the Kid in Santa Fe?

There are two plaques in Santa Fe pointing out where Billy the Kid spent jail time in 1880–1881. Look for plaques on the Cornell Building at 208 W. San Francisco and Otra Vez Building at 202 Gallisteo Street (now housing the Collected Works Books Store). Despite being seen as glamorous by some, Billy the Kid, also known as William Bonney, was a robber and a killer. None of his shootings or gambling seems to have taken place in Santa Fe. He reportedly washed dishes at the La Fonda Hotel. Hey, being a robber and sure shot doesn't always pay the rent. Today he would probably be paid residuals on the sale of Billy the Kid Sarsaparilla, available around town.

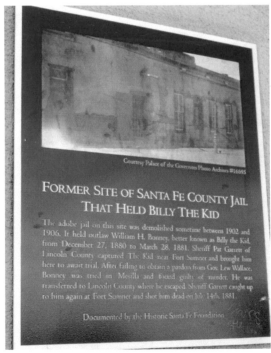

Billy the Kid plaque. Courtesy Pat Hodapp.

49. Visit International Folk Art Festival

The internationally heralded Folk Art Festival (www.fol-kartalliance.org) takes place on Museum Hill the week after the 4th of July and features hundreds of folk artists from around the world. Don't miss the parade of flags that kicks off the event—it is as thrilling as the Olympics parade of countries' flags. It is easy to get to, as the organizers provide free buses with your ticket from key downtown locations for the ten minute ride to the Milner Plaza on Museum Hill. Until you have been to one of these joyful, international gatherings, you don't know what you have been missing.

850 artists from 92 countries have taken part since 2003. Meeting these exceptional artists who come from developing countries connects you in a personal, heartfelt way. They bring much needed funds back to their communities, which impacts their daily lives.

Devi Karna of Nepal at Folk Art Festival. Courtesy Folk Art Festival Alliance and Bob Smith.

48. Get Your History Fix

The Palace of the Governors (105 W. Palace Ave.; www.palaceofthegovernors.com), situated on the north side of the Plaza was built in 1610. This palace is an adobe building—no turrets and golden spires. It is the oldest continuously used public building in the United States. It has flown many flags — Spanish, Mexican, Confederate and the Territorial flag of New Mexico before it became a state. If the Pueblo Native Americans who occupied Santa Fe after the 1680 Pueblo Revolt had had a flag, that would have been six flags that flew there! The most famous governor was Lew Wallace, author of *Ben Hur*. Take the opportunity to shop from the Indian merchandise spread on blankets before each artist under the portal at the front of the Palace of the Governors on the Plaza. Every day, Native Americans come from their pueblos and reservations from across the state to sell their wares. What is special is that you meet the artists under the portal. Don't expect to barter; the prices are already more than fair.

Explore the New Mexico History Museum (113 Lincoln Ave.; www.nmhistorymuseum.org) on the Plaza. From Native American tribes and pueblos to Spanish conquerors and trains, the museum exhibits cover it all. Check for special events "Behind the Blue Door" on Lincoln Street, just north of the Plaza. In summer, mountain men rendezvous and children of the portal artists hold special events for the public in the grassy courtyard. Free talks are scheduled regularly in their auditorium and meeting rooms. Check their calendar for events.

Native American artisans selling jewelry under the Palace of the Governors Portal. Courtesy Barbe Awalt.

59

47. Celebrate the Holidays!

There are many holiday festivities at the NM History Museum (113 Lincoln Ave.; www.nmhistorymuseum.org), on the Plaza. Around Christmas, they host a Holiday Night for families. Entering by the Blue Door on Lincoln Street, just north of the Plaza, children of all ages flock to sing along with local choirs and music. Santa Claus holds court in the courtyard. An old printing press from the 1800s is set to work printing Christmas cards for all who attend. Cider, *biscochitos* and *luminarias* make it a magic, non–commercial night with the true feeling of Christmas past.

Walk *Las Posadas,* a northern New Mexico tradition, on the Plaza the weekend before Christmas. Members of a local church lead the procession with traditional songs as they walk behind Joseph and Mary as they try to find a place to stay the night. Complimentary candles are given out and everyone turns to a neighbor to light their candle before the procession begins. Slowly the procession starts around the Plaza, and then a devil shows himself on a balcony and shouts in Spanish for Mary and Joseph to move on. The crowd boos the devil! The procession moves to each side of the Plaza and again they are turned away with rude swearing from the devil. At last, the procession reaches the blue doors of the History Museum. Suddenly the doors open and Mary and Joseph are allowed in. Everyone flocks into the courtyard where *luminarias* (bonfires) are lit and hot cider and biscochitos are served to all in the courtyard. The smoke from the *luminarias* mixes with the aroma of hot cider and all begin to sing Spanish and English carols.

Walk the Canyon Road Christmas Eve *Farolito* Walk — *farolitos* are small paper bags with sand in the bottom to hold a small candle. They are called *luminarias* elsewhere, but calling them *farolitos* helps you pass as a local. Over 10,000 *farolitos* light up the one-mile walk, with 25,000 people walking between dusk and midnight. You will find yourself in a holiday mood as people stop to sing carols around a *luminaria* fire.

One year, getting out of the crowd, my family took a short cut down a side street. There before us were a group of four or five people handing out posole, biscochitos and an agave punch to all who came down the snow-packed street. The real surprise was that the hosts of this table outside an adobe home were friends from Denver. We both had traveled 450 miles to celebrate Christmas Eve in Santa Fe, not knowing the other was going to be there too! And the food? Cooked by legendary Sam'l Arnold of the Fort restaurant in Denver, CO. Serendipity at its best in Santa Fe. Don't pooh, pooh it!

Las Posadas on the Plaza. Courtesy The New Mexico History Museum.

46. Watch the Christmas Tree Lighting on the Plaza

The day after Thanksgiving, the city turns on the Plaza holiday lights and lights the Christmas tree. After brief remarks from politicos, the lights burst upon the darkened Plaza. Christmas carols ring from the bandstand and Santa arrives in an old fire truck decked with holiday lights. Mr. and Mrs. Santa are available for a selfie and Santa sports a lighted sombrero. Packed shoulder to shoulder, Santa Feans meet and greet old friends and neighbors. It ends just in time to make that dinner reservation at a downtown restaurant.

Christmas lights on the Plaza. Courtesy City of Santa Fe Communications/ Multi-Media Office.

45. Inhale the Aroma of Great Coffee

There is good coffee, and there is great coffee. Locals love their coffee and those shops that sell the best. Ohori's (505 Cerrillos Rd. and 1098½ S. St. Francis; www.ohoriscoffee.com) is a Santa Fe favorite, started by a young woman just out of college, it has grown into having more than one location. C.G. Higgins (130 Lincoln Ave.; www.CGHigginsChocolates.com) touts their family grown, hand–picked coffee from Guatemala—organic and fair trade. They know the growers personally. ECCO (128 E. Marcy St.; www.eccogelato.com) has great baristas and locally roasted coffee—they make the coffee the way you ask. A faux mocha you say? No hassle, no wait. All have staff who can paint the Mona Lisa in the foam on your latte or mocha with a flair, well at least flowing leaves and flowers. Check out Downtown Subscription, Java Joe's, Iconik, Tribes, 35° North, … and more. Find your own favorite local coffee shop—Santa Fe has dozens.

Latte. Courtesy Pat Hodapp.

44. Love your Dog!

Dogs rule in Santa Fe, from Assistance Dogs of the West to your above average pet. (Oh, that's right, NO dog is average in Santa Fe.) Pamper your pets at TecaTu (www.tecatu.com) in the De Vargas Mall—clothes to food to special treats. Businesses put out bowls for water for thirsty dogs. Keep dogs on a leash unless you are at the Frank Ortiz Dog Park (1160 Camino de Las Crucitas; www.Bringfido.com)—38 acres to run around in and meet Santa Fe's best. Sorry, most large festivals on the Plaza do not allow pets, just assistance miniature ponies and assistance dogs.

Blackey at off-leash park. Courtesy Fred Friedman.

43. Indulge at the Wine & Chile Fiesta

A winning combination – wine and chile! 100 world–class wineries and 75 local restaurants showcase Santa Fe's best each September at the Santa Fe Wine & Chile Fiesta (www.santafewineandchile.org). Guest chefs host luncheons, give demonstrations, wine seminars and a grand reception at the Santa Fe Opera. Chile is a main ingredient in the special dishes offered, matched with the best wine choices. Historically, Santa Fe was the first U.S. city to make wine, and the state boasts 60 wineries. Wine making has come a long way from the first grapevines brought to New Mexico in about 1629 by Spanish monks, who fermented grapes for their own wine for communion.

Santa Fe Wine & Chile Fiesta logo. Courtesy Santa Fe Wine & Chile Fiesta.

42. Experience the Santa Fe Opera

The Santa Fe Opera (301 Opera Dr.; www.Santafeopera. org) is world renowned. The setting is as amazing as the operas that are presented. Just fifteen minutes north of Santa Fe, the operas are presented from late June through August. Not sure you like opera? Then attend the Opera Apprentices shows at the end of the season. The apprentices sing their hearts out to an appreciative audience and scouts from major operas looking for talent. Inexpensive, you can attend with your whole family. Don't forget to take part in the Opera tradition of having a tailgate dinner in the parking lot by your car. Watching the opera goers with their fine china and crystal glasses serving up gourmet meals prior to the performance adds to the glamor of the evening. Watching the sunset on the hills is just a prelude to the great operas presented. Only the heartiest of opera lovers will buy standing room only tickets for the back of the audience, but at the very discounted price, many do it. No matter what the daytime temperature is, bring a coat or shawl and the most cautious bring a raincoat. The Opera House is partially open to the elements.

Santa Fe Opera. Courtesy Barbe Awalt.

41. Stop by Burro Alley

Long the destination of traders and the military's mules, early Santa Feans came to Burro Alley to purchase wood hauled in from the hills on the burros. Located between Palace Avenue and San Francisco Streets, Burro Alley features restaurants today. Burro Alley has a mascot sculpture which is a favorite photo stop today. Rub his ears for good luck, but be careful of the tail. Two tails have had to be replaced due to rambunctious kids hanging on it.

Burro Alley donkey. Courtesy Pat Hodapp.

40. Visit the San Francisco de Assisi Statue

Outside City Hall in front of apricot trees, Saint Francis contemplates a small prairie dog at his feet in the statue by Andrea Bacigalupa. Benches have been placed for quiet contemplation. Locals sometime dress the prairie dog with a scarf and cap to keep it warm in the winter. Librarians seem to be the prime suspects.

St. Francis of Assisi statute in front of City Hall at Lincoln and Marcy Streets. Courtesy Pat Hodapp.

39 Salute the Sgt. Leroy Petry Statue

A statue of New Mexico's most famous Medal of Honor winner was created by sculptor and former Pojoaque Pueblo Governor George Rivera to honor Sgt. Petry for his bravery in Afghanistan where he lost his hand while saving his troops. The statue's artificial hand has been cast with a silver tone. Soldiers and families come to see the statue and touch the silver hand to thank Sgt. Petry for his gallantry.

Sgt. Leroy Petry statue in front of City Hall at Lincoln and Marcy Streets. Courtesy Pat Hodapp.

38. Walk Among a School of Cutthroat Trout

We may be in the desert in New Mexico, but we love our streams where all species of trout tempt fishermen. This whimsical sculpture installation by Colette Hosmer has 27 Rio Grande cutthroat trout all poking their heads up at the same time as if doing an Olympic swim routine. These trout are granite, and people gravitate to them to feel the smooth rock. The City Arts Commission has 75 permanent pieces on display throughout the City.

"Santa Fe Current" Cutthroat Trout sculpture next to the Santa Fe Community Convention Center. Courtesy Pat Hodapp

37. You'll Want to Eat a Baker's Dozen!

You will want to order a baker's dozen of these great pastry treats—that is 13, by the way. Locals drool just at the name Chocolate Maven (821 W. San Mateo Rd.; www.chocolatemaven.com), a bakery and restaurant that caters to your favorite baked goods. Be sure to order ahead if you are planning goodies for a birthday party or dinner party. Don't be put off by the industrial look of the building, the treasures are inside! When I was in Santa Fe for a job interview, the interviewer took me to Chocolate Maven for lunch. I was told I was a shoe-in as I was the only candidate taken to Chocolate Maven after the interview. Yes, I got the job. Then there is Angel's Bakery & Café (125 E. Water St.). Oh my. They bake for many of the restaurants and grocery stores in town—don't miss their famous *tres leches* cake and *empanadas*. Or if you are looking for biscochitos, the beloved official state cookie of New Mexico, Angel's is the place. One of my volunteers declared that they looked like something Jane Austen would have had on her tea table! Clafouti's (402 N. Guadalupe St.) has the market on croissants of every kind—but good luck finding a parking space!

Angel's Bakery & Cafe. Courtesy Barbe Awalt.

36. Celebrate La Fiestas

Fiestas celebrates the Spanish re-taking of Santa Fe and northern New Mexico from the Pueblo Indians and features many community events. In early September, watch the crowning of the Fiesta Queen, welcome Don Diego De Vargas and their Royal Court, see a children's pet parade and giggle at the participants in the Historical /Hysterical Parade; all of Santa Fe takes part. Thousands line the parade route to see horses, floats and marching bands. Mariachi concerts and strolling Mariachis set the tone of the festival. *Viva la Fiesta!* can be heard all weekend. Watch the Entrada on the Friday of Fiestas on the Plaza. Costumed locals portray Don Diego De Vargas and his men, and the Reina and her Court are present. The short pageant is presented in Spanish.

The *Defile de Los Niños*, better known as the Pet Parade, features children with their pets. Anyone can enter the parade, as long as they have a child with them, and there are bragging rights for winners in many categories, such as for most original costume, best theme plus dozens more. And the pets range from llamas to iguanas as well as costumed dogs and cats. An out-of-town friend so wanted to enter her dog she was soliciting for a child to walk with her! A purrfect parade to watch. Judging takes place on the Plaza.

Just a note, La Fiesta rules still include "no horses are allowed in the La Fonda Hotel Lobby."

Children in traditional costumes. Courtesy City of Santa Fe Communications/Multi-media Office.

La Fiesta celebration. Courtesy Pat Hodapp.

73

35. Ring in the New Year!

Celebrate the New Year on the Plaza! Join the throngs of party goers on the Plaza to hear music from the bandstand, sip hot beverages and warm up around glowing *luminaria* bonfires. Messages of hope and resolutions for the next year can be written on boards around the Plaza by the celebration goers. Traditional *farolitos*, small paper bags with sand holding a lit candle, line the sidewalks and the city's holiday tree lights glow until it is time for the countdown. Then all the lights go out and the mayor starts the countdown with everyone joining in...10, 9, 8, 7, 6, 5, 4, 3, 2, 1! A red glowing Zia symbol rises slowly above the Catron building, glowing over Santa Fe. The Zia Pueblo gave permission for the city to use its sacred symbol of the sun for this celebration. Happy New Year!

New Years' Eve on the Plaza. Courtesy Chelsey Evans.

34. Explore Buffalo Thunder Art

Few people know about the extensive Native American art collection at Buffalo Thunder Resort and Casino. (20 Buffalo Thunder Trail; www.bufffalothunderresort.com) The casino hosts nearly 400 pieces of incredible art. Buffalo Thunder is 20 minutes north of Santa Fe on the Pojoaque Pueblo. Shuttles to Buffalo Thunder from the Santa Fe Railrunner Depot are free. Noted artist and sculptor George Rivera's art is featured. Walk into the hotel and be greeted by dozens of sculptures, pots and paintings. An 8 foot by 8 foot painting by Hopi artist Dan Naminga dominates a hallway; I have hinted to Mr. Naminga that a daring heist might net me the painting – but then where to hang it? Ask for a tour of their art, which graces the entrance way and halls. The art will take your breath away.

Buffalo Thunder Resort and Casino Governor's Suite. Courtesy New Mexico Tourism Department.

33. Visit the Oldest House & Church

The oldest house in the United States (215 E. De Vargas St.; www.belltowerpropertiessantafe.com/about-santa-fe/general/oldest-house/) was constructed circa 1646, but has ties back to 1598. See what it was like to live in Santa Fe in the 17th century. No thanks, I think I'll stay in the 21st century with conveniences.

The Oldest House. Courtesy Pat Hodapp.

Next door is the oldest church in the United States, San Miguel Mission Church (401 Old Santa Fe Trail; www.sanmiguelchapel.org) which was remodeled in 2013, with volunteers making 70-pound adobe building blocks. The walls of the interior feature a gilded statue of St. Michael, the patron saint of the Franciscan brothers, brought from Mexico in 1709. Animal hides with religious paintings on them hang on the walls. The late Father Lester gave spirited tours of the church, pointing out the carved beam and the tanned animal hide portraits. He never left out the story of the first Indians to help build the church. They, according to church history, are buried under the church. Father Lester always ended his tour with the tale of tourists seeing a line of Indians walk across before the altar one summer day. The church is home to many musical concerts. Go very early on Christmas Eve if you want to get into the Church for Medieval chants and sacred music by Schola Cantorum or possibly an early Mass.

San Miguel Mission Church. Courtesy Pat Hodapp.

32. Listen to the Santa Fe Chamber Music Festival

Musicians come from all over the world to take part in this mid–July through August festival. International, world class musicians such as Pinchas Zuckerman and Itzak Perlman have performed. The locals' secret is that the musicians practice in the St. Francis Auditorium in the NM Museum of Art (107 W. Palace Ave.;www.nmartmuseum.org) almost every day they are in Santa Fe. Picture this: your free seats are in row 7 center, and Itzak Perlman is on stage holding a master class with a very talented young musician. Yes, it is free. Check the bulletin board at the St. Francis Auditorium for schedules. Of course you can then go to the full concerts later in the week.

New Mexico Museum of Art. Courtesy Pat Hodapp.

31. Bring Roses to the Santuario de Guadalupe

Built as a shrine for the Virgin of Guadalupe in 1781, the Santuario de Guadalupe (100 S. Guadalupe St.; www.santafe.com/article/santuario-de-guadalupe) was remodeled in 2006. Entering the church, one steps over a beam and has to bend down as it is a little door. Legend has it that entering in humble posture was to guarantee your paying homage to God. Others say that posture made any unwanted guests easier to keep out. Church services are only held on Saturday mornings; the church has many santos and paintings. Check with the church for occasional concerts held in the Santuario or its next-door modern church. In response and protest to an artist painting the Virgin of Guadalupe in a polka dot bikini, the church raised funds to have a sculpture made and shipped from Mexico. The twelve foot metal sculpture of Our Lady of Guadalupe stands next to the Santuario. Even in winter the faithful bring flowers, including the traditional roses, to place at her feet. Local wags have created "In Guad We Trust" bumper stickers.

The Virgin of Guadalupe statue at the Santuario. Courtesy Pat Hodapp.

30. Retrace Route 66

Old Route 66, which was aligned through Santa Fe from 1926–1937, is a 2,448-mile highway that has become a destination for those following the old highway that went across America from Chicago, IL to Santa Monica, CA. Long referred to as the great highway, John Steinbeck named this the "Mother Road" in *Grapes of Wrath*, telling of farmers coming from the Dust Bowl to try to find jobs in California. Those of a certain era learned of Route 66 from the TV program of the same name. As teens, we envied the freedom of George Maharis and the late Martin Milner as they took to Route 66 in their Corvette convertible. Traveling Route 66 today is a favorite vacation for students, and us older types, for people from Germany to South Korea and Japan. Watch for signage that identifies the Historical Route 66. The Historical 1926–1937 route went from Old Pecos Trail down over La Bajada Hill (now on I–25) into Albuquerque.

Route 66 vanity license plate. Courtesy Pat Hodapp.

29. Seek Out An Allan Houser Sculpture

Allan Houser, Apache sculptor and painter, has his sculptures all around Santa Fe. Take time to seek them out—at the Museum of Indian Art and Culture on Museum Hill, by the State Capitol Roundhouse, and the Santa Fe Botanic Garden, there are about 30 around the city. Stop by the Allan Houser Gallery (125 Lincoln Ave.; www.allanhouser.com) to see drawings and smaller pieces. Born Chiricahua Apache, Mr. Houser's father fought along with Geronimo. As a nephew of Geronimo, he heard first hand from his family of the difficult times of Native Americans in the West. His art depicts such scenes as "Lament," "Forever," and "When Friends Meet." Be sure to visit his sculpture studio south of Santa Fe.

Allan Houser sculpture at the NM Museum of Art. Courtesy Barbe Awalt.

28. Book 'em!

The owners of Collected Works Bookstore and Coffee-house (202 Galisteo St.; www.collectedworksbookstore.com), have made this independent book store a destination for book lovers from all over the state and country. Hosting hundreds of authors every year, the cozy store echoes with the words of poets and prose authors. On any given day you can hear, and meet, such well known authors as Hampton Sides, Michael McGarrity, Anne Hillerman, James McGrath Morris, Nasario Garcia or first-time authors and poets, in addition to such musical treats as harp and dulcimer concerts. Enjoy a coffee of your choice or fresh-baked goods while surrounded by books. Pretty close to being what I think Heaven should be. Other bookstores in Santa Fe include Op.Cit. Books (De Vargas Mall; www.opcitbooks.com), which also has used books, and Garcia Street Books (376 Garcia St.; www.garciastreetbooks.com). Don't overlook the great book stores in the city's museums (www.museumfoundation.org/shops)—often they host selections of travel and historical books found nowhere else. Santa Fe knows how to "book 'em."

Lorene Mills (left) and Sandra Cisneros. Courtesy Collected Works Bookstore and Coffeehouse.

27. Show your Pride

The Gay Pride Festival (www.santafehra.org) and parade take place on the fourth weekend of June. Floats, music groups and costumed marchers join in the GLBTQ celebration on the Plaza. Then in August, take in the Gay Rodeo, the Zia Regional Rodeo, at the Rodeo Grounds. Events abound all year round. Check out the Human Rights Alliance website for up-to-date calendar listings, which include plays, dances and benefit parties.

Gay Pride flag. Courtesy Pat Hodapp.

26. Go Back in Time at El Rancho de las Golondrinas

El Rancho de las Golondrinas (334 Los Pinos Rd.; www.golondrinas.org), which means Ranch of the Swallows, is just south of Santa Fe. It is a living history museum on a colonial ranch founded in 1710. Originally this 200-acre former ranch was the last camping place on the Camino Real, the road north from Mexico City, before travelers reached Santa Fe. As it is a living history ranch, visitors step back centuries into a lost time of farming and colonial life. Period-costumed volunteers and staff work at the ranch just as the founders did. Make bread, shear sheep, milk the cows, shoe horses and take part in spinning wool and the everyday life of colonial settlers. In addition, Las Golondrinas is known for its festivals. The Harvest Festival, Wine festival and Renaissance Fair bring hundreds of families to the site. A hands–on camp for all ages during the summer is a great way to learn ranch life. As I lived on a farm in the 1950s, it is nostalgic for me to visit Las Golondrinas.

El Rancho de las Golondrinas. Courtesy Barbe Awalt.

25. Sneak a Peek!

You'll be green with envy touring homes in Santa Fe. Enjoy the houses in these special tours; many are old original adobes as well as modern styles. Go beyond adobe walls to see Santa Fe show homes and gardens. Show House (www.showhousesantafe.com) opens homes to visitors two weekends in October. Behind Adobe Walls (www.thesantafegardenclub.org) takes place in July. One tour member in a particular home was heard to exclaim, "Oh, that is so Georgia" referring to Georgia O'Keeffe's sense of style.

Santa Fe home. Courtesy New Mexico Tourism Department.

24. Red or Green?

Even the TV show *Jeopardy* asked its contestants, "Red or green is the state question of what U.S. state? " Of course, the answer is "What is New Mexico!" Made official by the NM State Legislature in 1998, the question refers to your choice of red or green chile when ordering your food. Today, the "in" answer to red or green is Christmas, which means both red and green. Almost too cute. In late summer into fall, in shopping centers and on corner lots, you can smell the roasting chiles and hear the whoosh of the propane flames in the huge, rotating barrels. Few can resist the appeal of fresh roasted chiles to put in stews or on a slice of Indian bread. The number one chile is Hatch's, from Hatch, NM. After the airlines tightened their rules on luggage, many Santa Feans had to become creative to ship fresh green chile to home-sick college students or friends who had left New Mexico. Soldiers on military duty around the world asked for their Hatch's green chiles. If you peel your own, know that the minute you have chile oil on your hands your nose will itch and you will forget and rub your eyes…never fails. You'd think you would remember from year to year, but nooo.

Red or Green chile? Courtesy Pat Hodapp.

23. Dance to Music on the Plaza

What would you like to hear? Zydeco? Country? Marimba? It will likely be in the Plaza Bandstand Music Summer Series (www.Santafebandstand.org). Sponsored by the City of Santa Fe, the Plaza has music most noon hours and at dusk at the bandstand starting in early July and going through August. Chairs circle the front of the bandstand, as people begin to arrive. The first one on the dance floor for years was a friend, who grabbed his wife and they danced everything joyously. Now his friends dance for him. Follow the saying, "dance as if nobody is looking." Keith did, and so can you.

Plaza dancers. Courtesy David Goldberg.

22. Hear Lannan Foundation Talks

The Lannan Foundation (www.lannan.org/programs), a family foundation, sponsors "Readings and Conversation," a series of programs which bring nationally and internationally recognized poets and writers to Santa Fe to read and discuss their work in a public setting. They also sponsor a series called *In Pursuit of Cultural Freedom*, a lecture series featuring philosophers, writers, scholars, and social justice activists discussing political, economic, environmental, and human rights issues. The series typically begins each September and runs through May the following year. In keeping with their desire to make the programs available to all, tickets are under $10 and the programs are held at the Lensic. Be aware very popular and well-known authors and political activists' talks can sell out in minutes. Hopefuls are known to line up for a block outside the Lensic to get tickets.

Lannan Foundation. Courtesy Pat Hodapp.

21. Help Burn Zozobra

Old Man Gloom (www.burnzozobra.com) was originally created by Santa Fe artist Will Shuster as an entertainment for his friends. Over the years, Zozobra has grown into a 50-foot, 2,000-pound puppet who is burned to take all your gloom with him. The burning takes place the week before Fiestas in September, but the night varies. Zozobra is stuffed with paper, and a space is kept for adding your "gloom" messages to be burned. People have burned divorce papers, bad report cards and thousands of bad feelings in the Old Man. Held at Fort Marcy Park, which opens in the afternoon for Zozobra goers. Music and dancing precedes the actual burning, which elicits the screams of "Burn him, Burn him!" It is a mob scene as about 30,000 people attend. Me, I watch it on a local TV station.

Burning of Zozobra. Courtesy City of Santa Fe Communications/Multimedia Office.

20. Visit Galleries All Around Town

With hundreds of galleries in Santa Fe, finding ones that appeal to you is easy! Niman Gallery (125 Lincoln Ave.; www.namingha.com) features three of my favorite Hopi artists—Dan, Michael, and Arlo Namingha, who work in oils, acrylics, graphic art and wood/stonework sculptures. They recently celebrated their 25th year at this gallery. Don't miss Nedra Matteucci's gallery and sculpture gardens (1075 Paseo de Peralta; www.matteucci.com). Her gallery is legendary in Santa Fe for the gallery art and sculpture gardens, which is a magical place to enjoy art and sit and watch the koi in the ponds in lazy, late afternoons. InArt (319 Delgado St.; inartssantafe.com) features contemporary art and hosts the New Mexico plein air artists' annual exhibition. Sorrelsky Gallery (125 W Palace Ave.; www.sorrelsky.com) brings contemporary Indian art and jewelry to a welcoming space on East Palace Avenue. All feature special openings with the artists. Don't stop there; cruise Washington Avenue, San Francisco and Delgado Streets in addition to Canyon Road. You won't be disappointed.

Nedra Matteucci Galleries sign. Courtesy Pat Hodapp.

19. Ride the Rails

Spot the Santa Fe caboose at the intersection of St. Francis Drive and Cerrillos Road. It has become the most photographed object in Santa Fe! In 2015 train lovers saved the caboose from being sold. Many donations were made in the name of Abe Silver, Jr., an avid train lover. It is believed to be a Denver and Rio Grande Western caboose from the 1940s or early 1950s. The rails it sits on were used by the New Mexico Central Railroad that ran from Tomasita's Restaurant all the way to El Paso, Texas. On the southside of Santa Fe, there is a spot where two sets of rails diverge—one set are from the 1880s and the other are modern commuter train tracks. Santa Fe was a destination of the Atchison, Topeka and the Santa Fe Railroad, but passenger train service for Santa Fe only lasted a few years. The closest depot to take Amtrak is 20 minutes away in Lamy. Only the Railrunner commuter train and the Santa Fe Southern Sunset & Stargazing Train Ride come into Santa Fe these days. Catch the Railrunner for a ride to Albuquerque and points south. The Sunset-Stargazing train ride runs Wednesdays to Sundays. For a longer train ride, take the Toltec and Cumbres ride out of Chama, two hours north of Santa Fe, where a steam locomotive cuts through the hills and forest.

Denver and Rio Grande Western caboose. Courtesy Pat Hodapp.

18. Soak Your Cares Away

One Thanksgiving over 25 years ago, my husband and I flew to Santa Fe on a whim. Forgetting it was ski season, we stopped at Ten Thousand Waves (3451 Hyde Park Rd.; www.tenthousandwaves.com) to soak in a heated pool. There was one private pool available, surrounded by coyote fencing and junipers. It was heaven to soak in the warm water in the sun as clouds moved by and it started to snow. Now with an in-house restaurant, Izanami to add to its rustic accommodations for rent, Ten Thousand Waves is a destination. Why would you ever have to leave? Just remember to make reservations early, particularly in the winter months.

A local favorite for hot springs is Ojo Caliente, about an hour northwest of Santa Fe.

Ten Thousand Waves. Courtesy Pat Hodapp.

17. Seek Out Western Hats, Boots & Jewelry

If you plan to buy a new hat in Santa Fe, scuff it up a bit, bend the brim and even throw a little dust on it. Same with new boots – pristine boots with no dust or cow pie on them yell "TOURIST!" Turquoise and silver are beautiful in moderation. Two squash blossom necklaces, two silver rings and three bracelets being worn all at once draw chuckles from locals. One Indian Market, a Midwesterner almost fell over forward due to the weight of her newly purchased silver and turquoise which about blinded a passersby in the noon day sun. Now, I am not picking on Midwesterners; I was born in Michigan myself, I am just suggesting a little restraint.

Santa Fe has a casual western look all its own. Worn jeans, denim shirts, suede jackets, broomstick skirts (and concho belts on everyone), and don't forget the boots. Take a look at Back at the Ranch Cowboy Boots (209 Marcy St.; www.back-attheranch.com). Rio Bravo Trading Company (411 Guadalupe St.; www.riobravotradingcompany.blogspot.com/) features old and new cowboy collectibles, try on a Charlie One Horse hat—you won't be able to go home without it. Double Take (319 S. Guadalupe St.; www.santafedoubletake.com) is consignment and new western wear.

Rio Bravo Trading Company. Courtesy Pat Hodapp.

16. Don't Pick Datura!

Almost any dry, sandy spot including street dividers will have flourishing Datura plants. Made famous by Georgia O'Keeffe, this white, trumpet-shaped flower only blooms at dusk and lasts only until the next day. Also known as Jimson Weed, the plant is poisonous to livestock, despite its innocent look. Often called Sacred Datura, the plant's five to seven inch trumpet–like flower is held together with little points on the petals, which slowly detach as it blooms. Some claim if you have two or more margaritas and sit close to the Datura, you can hear a little "pip" as the petals detach to bloom.

Sacred Datura in bloom. Courtesy Pat Hodapp.

15. Look at New Mexico License Plates

New Mexico is the only state in the Union to have "USA" on its license plates. Even that does not keep people from thinking New Mexico is the country of Mexico. Many tales of not receiving mail or residents not being able to order from a catalog "because the store does not ship out of the country" are numerous. Every Santa Fean will share their own story of whether they convinced the clerk or just had to give up explaining that NEW MEXICO is a state! So many stories of mistakes are told, some have become urban legends. My all time favorite is an elementary school teacher writing to the mayor asking for "sample money and stamps for her students so they could more identify with New Mexico." No one knows what the mayor's response was, but we're sure it was polite and not condescending. I wonder how much money he sent...

New Mexico license plate featuring USA. Courtesy Pat Hodapp.

14. Lights! Camera! Action!

Making movies and TV shows is becoming a big part of the Santa Fe street scene. The great weather, the backdrop of the Plaza, dirt roads in town, and old adobe buildings make for good filming. Even the local La Farge Branch Library was made up to be the sheriff's office in the TV program *Longmire*. Confused and upset library patrons called to find out exactly when was the library made into a sheriff's office; they wanted to return their books and the library was gone! If you see "Special Events Ahead" signs, it often means crews are blocking off streets and filming. Big, blocky signage with just initials on it, such as LM, means you can follow them to the set. Santa Feans are very protective of the celebrities' privacy. The library staff were so concerned that Russell Crowe would get a parking ticket when he parked in front of the library, they took turns watching and putting coins in the meter so he wouldn't get a ticket! That is Santa Fe hospitality.

Film crew at work. Courtesy City of Santa Fe Communications/Multi-media Office.

13. Meet the Birds at Audubon Center

Close to downtown, the Randall Davey Audubon Center (1800 Upper Canyon Rd.; www.nmaudubon.org) is an oasis of woods, open pasture and birds. All kinds of birds. Check online for details of guided bird walks, or just walk these easy trails by yourself. Many hummingbirds migrate through New Mexico. On one visit to Randall Davey, my friend had not seen one bird on the hike and was very peeved. Then as we walked between two of the buildings we could hear the distinctive buzz of hummingbirds, dozens of them. As we stepped into the sun we were between two hummingbird feeders and the hummingbirds just zoomed around us and one or two plopped into our red shirts. The hummingbirds were soft and felt like big raindrops as they hit. Their long slim bills were not sharp; we just hoped we did not bend them!

Randall Davey Audubon Center. Courtesy Pat Hodapp.

12. Take Santa Fe Home With You

Nothing reminds one of Santa Fe like a red ristra of chiles. Created in strings, and now wreaths, the ristras can be decoration or part of your New Mexican recipes. Hung outside a front door, they give the home a sign of welcome to guests. At homes that have many strings hung up in the sun, most likely they grew the chiles themselves. Regular red and multicolored pepper wreaths can be found at the Farmer's Market (Paseo de Peralta at Guadalupe; Saturdays 8:00am – 1:00pm) all fall.

Ristras of chiles. Courtesy Pat Hodapp.

11. Get Your Rodeo On!

The Rodeo de Santa Fe (3237 Rodeo Rd.; www.rodeode-santafe.org) is usually held the last weekend in June, at the rodeo grounds. Just like the Mexican vaqueros who started the idea of rodeo in the 1800's, the rodeo in Santa Fe is like a hometown event. There is mutton busting for little kids (if they stay on a sheep they can win prizes) and youth barrel racing. Horses are the king of the corral as they provide half of calf roping and barrel racing teams. The Saturday before the official rodeo, a rodeo parade wends its way through downtown Santa Fe highlighting the Miss Rodeo queens, 4-H horseback riders and the sheriff's posse. Don't leave the parade until you see the red eyes in the official rodeo mascot, a huge white bull with glowing red eyes.

Rodeo de Santa Fe. Courtesy City of Santa Fe Communications/Multimedia Office.

10. Laugh at Without Reservations Cartoons

Every day except Sunday, Santo Domingo/Kewa Native American Ricardo Caté (www.Ricardocate.com) entertains the world with his cartoons in *Without Reservations*, found in the *Santa Fe New Mexican* newspaper. We all know to look up in the right-hand corner of the comics page and do it instinctively with our morning coffee cup in our hand. With his on–going characters of the Chief and the General always doing battle in gentle yet probing ways, Caté skewers everyone, Indian, Anglo and Hispanic. To almost every Santa Fean, his cartoon is how you start your day laughing. Caté also has paintings of his most popular drawings.

Cartoonist Ricardo Caté with paintings. Courtesy Pat Hodapp.

9. Spot the Hollyhocks

Holy hollyhocks – some grow to ten feet tall, in colors from white to yellow to black. The dark blue–black and black hollyhocks are popular, as Georgia O'Keeffe grew them near her home. The skirted blossoms are a favorite flower for children to turn into little fairy's skirts. They were so popular to paint that a few years ago the hundreds of paintings of the flower against adobe walls were ubiquitous and considered kitsch. They are Santa Fe's unofficial flower.

Hollyhocks against an adobe wall. Courtesy Pat Hodapp.

8. Try This—It Is No Taos Lightning!

In the 1800s, local distilled "moonshine" liquor was known to locals as *Taos Lightning*. Today, check out local, high-quality distilleries and microbreweries. Pick your favorite microbrew beer or spirits in town. Second Street Brewery (114 2nd St. and 1607 Paseo de Peralta; www.secondstreet-brewery.com) has great microbrews at two locations; I prefer the Railyard location to watch the Railrunner come and go. Santa Fe Brewery (35 Fire Pl.; www.santafebrewing.com) claims to be the oldest brewery in Santa Fe. It gives tours and has tasting rooms. Try their famous State Pen Porter and Santa Fe Nut Brown. Santa Fe Spirits (308 Read St.; www.santafespirits.com) owner Colin Keegan even brews apple brandy from his own apples and makes single malt whiskey and gin. Check out the tastings held at their Read Street and southside brewery on Mallard Way.

Santa Fe Spirits. Courtesy Pat Hodapp.

7. Watch for Coyotes, Deer and Bears, Oh My!

Santa Fe is a small urban center, surrounded by mountains and acres of grass. Our wild animal friends are attracted to our fields and yards. If you see what looks like a shaggy German Shepherd loping along your street, look again. It probably is a coyote. Coyotes make themselves known at night with howls and yips of delight when they catch something to eat or just dance in the moonlight. The deer manage to camouflage themselves well in parks and arroyos. As to bears, one was even found near Trader Joe's on Cordova Street. I think she wanted to shop.

Coyote. Courtesy Creative Commons.

6. Smell the Chamisa, NOT!

Starting in mid–summer, Chamisa, also known as rabbit-brush, starts to bloom beautiful, golden blossoms. The overall bush is a muted, light green that is very attractive along roads and in fields. Don't be like a newcomer who enthusiastically told her friends that she was picking Chamisa blossoms for her dinner party table and could not understand their laughter. As they sat down to dinner she realized the humor of the situation, for Chamisa blooms' aroma is that of an untended dog park. The friends helped her carry out the bushels of blossoms before enjoying dinner.

Chamisa in bloom. Courtesy Pat Hodapp.

5. Look for Mt. Baldy

Visitors are surprised to find Santa Fe surrounded by mountains, even though we are at 7,199 feet. Most prominent are the Sangre de Cristo mountains to the east of Santa Fe. Sunset on the mountains reflects a rosy pink to red glow that gave the Sangre de Cristo their name—Blood of Christ. In the Sangre de Cristo range, just northeast of Santa Fe, is Mt. Baldy, at 12,632 feet. Locals watch for the first snow on Mt. Baldy just as they look for the first apricot blossoms. It is an icon for Santa Fe. Now turn to the west to see the Jemez Mountains. Its tallest peak is Chicoma at 11,561 feet. Southwest of the City are the Ortiz mountains. Albuquerque's pride and joy are the Sandias which can be glimpsed from Santa Fe. Although not in Santa Fe, take the Albuquerque Sandia Peak tramway, the longest single span in the world—there is a restaurant at the top and hiking.

Mt. Baldy. Courtesy Pat Hodapp.

4. See WPA Art Everywhere

The 1930s Work Progress Administration (WPA) provided work for public buildings by artists during the Great Depression. New Mexico had 167 known artists compared to today's estimated 1,665 full time artists, writers, or performers. People claim that every other person in Santa Fe is an artist – and the other one is a writer. A little exaggeration. Santa Fe artists included William Penhallow Henderson, Pablita Velarde, Gene Kloss, Maria Martinez (of black pottery fame), Peter Hurd, Will Shuster (of Zozobra fame), Gerald Cassidy, and Fremont F. Ellis. Area coordinator was Gustave Baumann, a woodblock printer and marionette maker. Some of the best known works are two murals. Santa Fe's main post office (120 S. Federal Pl.) is graced with Gerald Cassidy's triptychs, and the U.S. Courthouse (106 S. Federal Pl.) has six huge landscapes painted by William Penhallow Henderson. Two stone sculptures by Hannah Small are at the entrance to the main library's lobby (145 Washington Ave.; www.santafelibrary.org). Some WPA art is still not identified, particularly the smaller pieces such as tinwork, furniture, colcha embroidery and pottery. I search Santa Fe's fabulous flea markets for WPA treasures. Of course, many WPA items belong to the US Government, but the search is the fun part.

Mural by Gerald Cassidy. Courtesy Barbe Awalt.

3. Pick the Apricots!

In a good year, Santa Fe will be bursting to the seams with apricot trees in bloom. As the fruit ripens the challenge is to pick when the apricots are ripe enough to eat, but not yet of interest to the birds and young children. Many people no longer pick the fruit and on some bike routes you will see bicyclists stopped, reaching up for a quick, sweet snack. If the fruit hangs over a fence or over a sidewalk, it is fair game. The apricot trees in front of City Hall at Marcy and Lincoln Street are usually particularly beautiful.

Apricots. Courtesy Pat Hodapp.

2. Make Snow People & Snow Buddhas

Snow is not that common, even though the city is at 7,000 feet. Pictures of snow men or kids making snow angels are still newsworthy. But one snowy December when I drove back into Santa Fe from a hard, long trip, I came across my neighbor's prized pickup truck with snow piled high on it. Down the street was a Snow Buddha with marigolds draped on its shoulders, feet in the lotus position and flowers in his snow bowl. A gentle sculpture to make you stop and think. Both so very Santa Fe.

Prized truck in snow. Courtesy Pat Hodapp.

1. Come Back to Santa Fe

I started a tradition with my many friends who have come to visit in Santa Fe. I give them a small, silver heart-shaped *milagro*, sold at shops and churches, and have them leave it in the church or bury it in Santa Fe with a wish to return. It guarantees you will come back to visit. *Milagros* come in all shapes to help you with the problem symbolized by the milagro. Heads, hearts, limbs and eyes are common forms. *Milagro* means miracle. Bury your *milagro* and come back to Santa Fe.

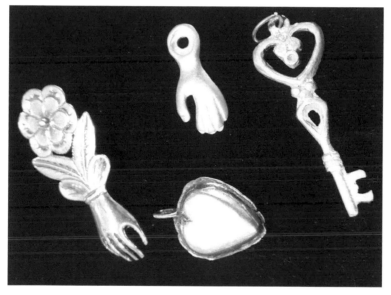

Milagros. Courtesy Pachamama/Lolly Martin.

Near Misses

If you're lucky enough to visit in the winter, catch the Glow at Santa Fe Botanic Garden – lights, music, hot drinks and seasonal fun. – *Anne Hillerman*

The Shed restaurant. Best red chile ever! My suggestion is smother everything in red! – *Steve Hansen*

Walk on Good Friday to the Santuario de Chimayo or just visit the church for holy healing soil to take home. – *Pat Hodapp*

Hike where O'Keeffe painted at Abiquiu and Ghost Ranch. See the flat topped Pedernal Mountain. – *Peggy Czyl*

Go to the celebration and Indian Market at Kewa/Santo Domingo Pueblo held every Labor Day. – *Ricardo Cate*

Relax and steam in the various super pools at Ojo Caliente Hot Springs. – *Jonathan Hodapp*

Madrid, New Mexico, is a magical town from the past.– *Mark & Mary Dunn*

Go to St. John's College campus for the talks and concerts.– *Jonathan Hodapp*

Enjoy the Chimayo Cocktail created by and served at Rancho de Chimayo. Apple juice and calvados with an apple slice. – *Steve Hansen*

I hope the Santa Fe Children's Museum reopens! – *Xavier, Isaiah and Maria Finley*

Drive on a dirt road; it'll take you back to days gone by and will bring out the cowboy in you. – *Pat Hodapp*

Watch a Fuego AAA baseball game at Fort Marcy Ball Park and watch the players play their hearts out for the love of the game. – *Jim Harlan*

Hike the Tent Rocks Kasha – Katuwe trail – amazing rock shapes. – *Jim Harlan*

Take a stroll or bike ride up Alameda on a late October day to enjoy the unique and colorful Santa Fe autumn. – *Bruce Adams*

Stand in the alignment of the old New Mexico Central Railroad, midway between the interstate and the community college at the flag stop of Donaciana, and listen to the locomotive stopping there, to sledge hammers on steel spikes and the laughter of ranch kids, up from Stanley and Moriarty, to Santa Fe for the day. – *Fred Friedman*

Wait in line and enjoy a Navajo Taco during Fiestas. – *Bruce Galpert*

Try a Margarita cocktail at Maria's, as they have one of the largest tequila menus in the world. Mmm, makes me thirsty in fact. – *Steve Hansen*

The autumnal drive up Hyde Park Road to the Santa Fe ski basin with the glorious, expansive views to the west and south, but especially Aspen Vista when the leaves of aspen trees shimmer like gold medallions on a sunny morning under the turquoise sky. – *Bev Friedman*

Stand on the north side of the plaza and read the inscription at the base of the obelisk at the center of the park. If you look carefully you will see that a word was erased from the marble by a chisel. Next walk around to the southern side and read the plaque added to the monument in 1973. Consider the missing word and reflect on the text of the newer plaque and in an instant you will have a lesson on New Mexico's struggles to come to terms with its past. – *James McGrath Morris*

Don't miss Horseman's Haven – hottest chile in New Mexico. Don't ask for the #2 unless you have an asbestos mouth, or be willing to be shamed for not eating it. – *Jonathan Hodapp*

Stop and smell the pinon – *Pat Hodapp*

A short drive to Tesuque's Shidoni Sculpture Gardens north of Santa Fe, coupled with a leisurely stroll through the grounds, will put you in touch with unique and aesthetically pleasing figures that range from the esoteric to the realistic. Each one individually and collectively will soothe your soul and even uplift your spirits if they're at a low ebb. – *Nasario Garcia, Ph.D.*

A day of visiting our consignment stores – best deals and best of the West in clothes, jewelry, hats and more. – *Susan Kilkenny*

Watch the monks making a sand Mandala at Seret's – it is magical and serene. – *Tim and Susan Kilkenny*

Harry's Road House has the best food and real road house atmosphere in the United States. – *Carol Evans, London*

Look for the Poetry in Motion Ice Cream Truck and move the GIANT poetry magnets around to spell out poetry and why you LOVE SANTA FE! – *Ilan Shamir*

Go to Rancho de Golondrinas with the King of Spain! – *Barbe Awalt*

Enjoy the winter wonderland experience of fresh snow on Atalaya Mountain. Embark as soon as possible after sunrise. – *Rebecca Wurzburger*

Check out the vast dog park on Camino Crucitas… walk into the arroyo and up a hill to see 360° views of the land and city.- *Mary-Charlotte Domandi*

Don't miss the Sweetwater Harvest Kitchen--any time, but Thursday night is Thai night. Don't take a chance, make a reservation! -*The Hodapp family*

Pick up a bacon & egg roll (with red chile) at Tia Sophia's. Portable deliciousness to get the day started!- *Laurie McGrath*

Visit the New Mexico History Museum with former Cultural Affairs Secretary Stuart Ashman. – *Barbe Awalt*

Tomasita's has the best sopapillas, hot at your table as you sit down! Oh, and stuffed sopapillas—try the beef with green chile.-*Pat Hodapp*

Experience Meow Wolf art collective's House of Eternal Return exhibit—100s of artists created it!- *K.M.*

Santa Fe Songs

Songs of Santa Fe
Lights of Old Santa Fe -- Roy Rogers and Dale Evans
Going to Santa Fe - Cadillac Bob
Santa-Fe - Bob Dylan
Surfin' Santa Fe Style - The Knights
Santa Fe - Beirut
Santa Fe Blues - Lightnin' Hopkins
Santa Fe - Newsies
Mean Old Santa Fe - Arthur "Big Boy" Crudup
Santa Fe - Bon Jovi
Santa Fe Fiesta Song - Turner, Palon and Valdes
Santa Fe - Rent
Hearts and Bones - Paul Simon
Lights of Santa Fe - Cathy Swinger (album)
Santa Fe - Michael Herrick
Santa Fe - Bellamy Brothers
Santa Fe Thief - Jimmie Dale
Santa Fe Lights - Sons of the San Joaquin
Christmas & Santa Fe - Ottmar Liebert (album)
Official Songs of Santa Fe - Ld Burke III (album)

Santa Fe Movies

Early films like Ride the Pink Horse show Santa Fe in 1947, whereas Crazy Heart filmed in 2009 portrays Santa Fe today. Most of the films made in Santa Fe feature cowboys and Indians, and in one case aliens!

In addition to the films set in Santa Fe, over 250 movies have been made in New Mexico. Filmmakers love the 300 days of sunlight, mountains, desert, ranches and fantastic clouds.

Crazy Heart - 2009
Lone Ranger - 2013
Santa Fe - 1951
Santa Fe - 1997
The Cowboy - 1958
Santa Fe Trail - 1940
Ride the Pink Horse - 1947
Sundown in Santa Fe - 1948
Cowboys and Aliens - 2011
The Cowboys - 1972
Manhattan-TV show - 2014
Longmire-TV - 2012-2016
Graves-TV - 2015

Indian Market in the Santa Fe Plaza. Courtesy Barbe Awalt.

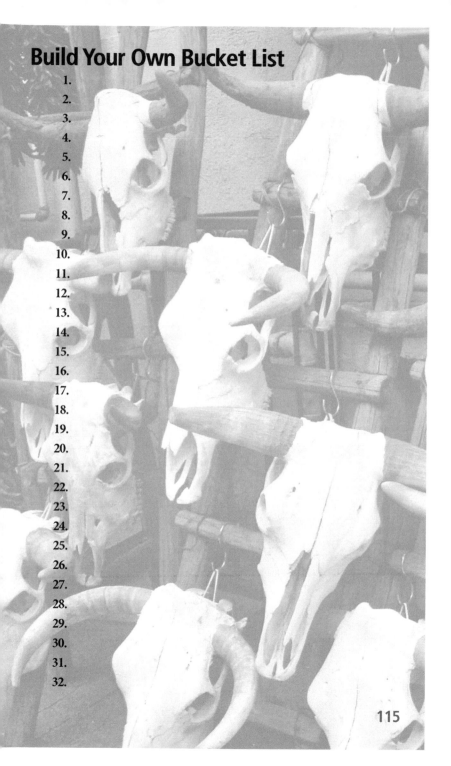

Build Your Own Bucket List

1.
2.
3.
4.
5.
6.
7.
8.
9.
10.
11.
12.
13.
14.
15.
16.
17.
18.
19.
20.
21.
22.
23.
24.
25.
26.
27.
28.
29.
30.
31.
32.

33.
34.
35.
36.
37.
38.
39.
40.
41.
42.
43.
44.
45.
46.
47.
48.
49.
50.
51.
52.
53.
54.
55.
56.
57.
58.
59.
60.
61.
62.
63.
64.
65.
66.

67.
68.
69.
70.
71.
72.
73.
74.
75.
76.
77.
78.
79.
80.
81.
82.
83.
84.
85.
86.
87.
88.
89.
90.
91.
92.
93.
94.
95.
96.
97.
98.
99.
100.

Santa Fe Public Library

The Santa Fe Public Library was founded in 1896 by the Woman's Club and Library Association. To support their library project, members sold lemonade on The Plaza!

The Library's key mission to support the Santa Fe community is still its ongoing goal. The Library provides our patrons with a public library with a large collection of books, programs, services, and materials that enrich the diverse community the Library serves. The Library serves patrons of all ages, families, students and life-long learners.

The Main Library and the two branches of the Santa Fe Public Libraries are community information hubs where everyone can gather to learn, create, and dream. The community through the Friends of the Library provide funding for top notch children's programs such as pre-school story times, Books and Babies, afterschool programs, homework help, Teen programs and the Summer Reading Program. These programs alone serve over 15,000 youth who come to the Libraries' programs annually. Funds for purchasing books and materials for all ages to support students and lifelong learners are raised through the community's generous support.

The Friends of the Library volunteers successfully hold multiple book sales each year of donated books and also run two used book stores, one at Southside Branch and one at the Main Library, to raise funds for Library needs. The Friends also hold special events to raise funds on behalf of the Library. Volunteers are the core of the Library and the Friends of the Library. We depend on these special friends who volunteer on behalf of the Library. Please consider volunteering for the Friends by contacting www.santafefriends.org/volunteer.html or call 505-955-2839. To volunteer for the Library, please call 505-955-6792 or go to our website www.santafelibrary.org .

To support the Library's children's programs and books, consider sending a check to: Santa Fe Public Library, 145 Washington Avenue, Santa Fe, NM 87501 Questions? www.santafelibrary.org or (505) 955-6789

Thanks for your generous support.

ABOUT THE AUTHOR

Pat Hodapp is the Director of Libraries for the City of Santa Fe. She is always exploring Santa Fe's myriad museums, art galleries, music, restaurants and those hidden gems behind coyote fences. She has been sharing "her city" with friends and visitors since 1973.

Courtesy Luis Sánchez Saturno.

Her gentle question to confused tourists on street corners, or in the middle of a street with a map or cell phone, is "Where are you heading?" This gives them a warm welcome to Santa Fe and helps lead them to their destination. Her favorite tourists include the many students and young people from around the world who are driving Route 66.

As a librarian at the Main Library downtown, many of the *100 Things to Do in Santa Fe Before You Die Bucket* List are items the tourists seek out information on, so it was easy to write about chocolate, coffee and where to get great New Mexican food! In addition to receiving the 2015 New Mexico-Arizona Book Awards' Literary Award in special recognition of her ongoing support for authors and books, Pat is an award-winning painter and baker.

CPSIA information can be obtained at www.ICGtesting.com
Printed in the USA
BVIW12n2349280417
482604BV00004B/11